Aspect-Oriented Programming with the *e* Verification Language

A Pragmatic Guide for Testbench Developers

David Robinson

AMSTERDAM · BOSTON · HEIDELBERG · LONDON
NEW YORK · OXFORD · PARIS · SAN DIEGO
SAN FRANCISCO · SINGAPORE · SYDNEY · TOKYO

ELSEVIER

Morgan Kaufmann is an imprint of Elsevier

Publishing Director: Joanne Tracy
Senior Acquisitions Editor: Chuck Glaser
Publishing Services Manager: George Morrison
Project Manager: Mónica González de Mendoza
Assistant Editor: Michele Cronin
Production Assistant: Lianne Hong
Composition: Charon Tec Ltd (A Macmillan Company)
Interior printer: Maple-Vail Book Manufacturing Group
Cover printer: Phoenix Color Corporation

Morgan Kaufmann Publishers is an imprint of Elsevier.
30 Corporate Drive, Suite 400, Burlington, MA 01803, USA

This book is printed on acid-free paper.

Library of Congress Cataloging-in-Publication Data
Robinson, David.
 Aspect-oriented programming with the e verification language : a pragmatic guide for testbench developers / David Robinson.
     p. cm.
 Includes bibliographical references and index.
 ISBN-13: 978-0-12-374210-0 (pbk. : alk. paper) 1. Object-oriented programming (Computer science) I. Title.
 QA76.64.R629 2007
 005.1′17 — dc22

                                   2007019636

ISBN: 978-0-12-374210-0

For information on all Morgan Kaufmann publications, visit our Web site at www.mkp.com or www.books.elsevier.com

Transferred to digital printing in 2009.

Working together to grow
libraries in developing countries

www.elsevier.com | www.bookaid.org | www.sabre.org

ELSEVIER   BOOK AID   Sabre Foundation
              International

Acknowledgments

I'd like to thank Ken Gray for making the innocuous comment that started the whole thing going in the first place. I'm fairly sure he meant it, but I sometimes can't help but feel that I've fallen for a large practical joke.

Keeping with the theme of innocuous comments for a moment, I'd like to thank Tommy Kelly for his very detailed review comments. During a phone conversation about some of these he just happened to mention that he had no idea what I was talking about by the end of the Introduction. That throw away line started one of the biggest rewrites the book ever had.

I'd like to thank Jason Sprott for stress testing my OOP arguments. As something of an OOP, Vera, SystemVerilog, testbench, and verification guru, having him admit that there might be a *slight possibility* that *maybe* AOP had *some kind* of an advantage over OOP on its own was a defining moment. I also have to thank Jason and Tommy for creating Verilab and inviting me in to play.

That leads me on nicely to thanking all the people (past and present) in Verilab for making it such a great place to work. The technical knowledge floating around in there is nothing short of amazing, and everyone has contributed to the making of this book. In particular, I'd like to thank Robert Fairlie, J.L. Gray, and Gordon McGregor for their detailed reviews.

Outside of Verilab, Suzanne Peggie, Claudia Blank, Mike Stellfox, Ernst Zwingenberger, Bernhard Klein, Robert Richter,

Christian Beckmann, John MacBeth, Gery Osowiecki, Andrew Piziali, and Thorsten Lutscher all deserve a special mention for helping make the book what it is — whether they realized it or not.

Finally, I'd like to thank Chuck Glaser, Monica Mendoza, Michele Cronin, and Dennis Schaefer at Morgan Kaufmann, and all the good folks at Charon Tec Ltd for actually making the book.

Table of Contents

Foreword

David Robinson has made a valuable contribution to the verification community with this book about Aspect-Oriented Programming (AOP) using *e*. Coverage-driven verification has entered the mainstream as a critical and central component of an effective verification methodology, and this has driven engineers to seek out the best practices for developing automated verification environments. There are many compelling reasons why people choose Specman Elite and the *e* language to tackle their verification problems — the declarative nature of the language which makes it easy to express stimulus constraints, temporal assertions, and functional coverage; the large library of predefined routines which make it easy to create sophisticated checkers and other testbench components; the flexibility provided by the extensibility of the language; or simply the fact that they find it to be an incredibly efficient way to get their job done. I have spent the last 8 years working with design and verification engineers to help them create constrained-random, coverage-driven verification environments using the *e* verification language. They don't usually start out saying, "I could really use an AOP language to make my verification work a lot easier…" In fact, most Specman experts and beginners who leverage the power of AOP in their everyday work to create and use *e* verification environments do so without much thought of exactly what AOP is all about. I, and other verification experts, have tried for many years to convey in simple terms the power of *e* as an AOP language to significantly simplify and accelerate the development of reusable, automated verification environments, but we have not succeeded in a way that matches the work David has created here. The success of hundreds of verification projects at many companies over the last ten years has shown that leveraging the AOP capabilities of *e* with a well-designed methodology can make it significantly easier to develop, use and reuse coverage-driven verification environments. Until David wrote this book based on his experiences as a verification engineer, there were not a lot of resources available for engineers and managers to learn about the advantages of using AOP with the *e* language. I really love the book … it provides very practical advice from David's years of real world experience. David's enjoyable writing style combined with his ability to clearly articulate deep technical concepts in simple terms make this book valuable to engineers and managers who know nothing about the *e* language and are trying to select a verification language for their next project, as well as to engineers who are very experienced users of *e* and want to learn more about how to leverage the power of AOP.

Preface

But when our hypothetical Blub programmer looks in the other direction, up the power continuum, he doesn't realize he's looking up. What he sees are merely weird languages. He probably considers them about equivalent in power to Blub, but with all this other hairy stuff thrown in as well. Blub is good enough for him, because he thinks in Blub.

Paul Graham [1]

Who is this book for?

It's for anyone who will read it. A *better* question might be, who will find this book useful? That would be verification engineers who are curious about this the aspect oriented programming (AOP) thing. In particular, you'll find this book useful if:

- You're an expert in object oriented programming (OOP) but wary about AOP because of what you've heard. It will show you that not only does AOP improve OOP and make software development easier, but it can do both of these without bringing an end to life as we know it.

- You're someone who uses AOP in your daily life but are not sure what it is you are using. Don't worry; no one else seems to know either. This book will explain what it is, show you when you should use it and when you shouldn't, and gives some useful tips about how to deal with it all.

■ You're someone who uses AOP in your job and are sure what it is you are using. Please get in touch. Hopefully, this book will give you some fresh ideas to try out, or at least be entertaining.

What is it about?

It's about aspect oriented programming. It doesn't just cover the academic stuff that you'll read about elsewhere, although that's useful, but also the more pragmatic side of AOP as well. It's about using AOP in ways that will make your code easier to write, easier to use, and easier to reuse. It's about using AOP in ways that will help you meet your project schedule.

It gives real examples of AOP in action and throws in some guidelines on how to organize your code so that you can actually find things again. Along the way, it describes what an aspect really is and why OOP isn't the panacea the Blub [1] programmers in our midst make out. It might even give you some ideas on how to avoid problems in OOP.

Why did I write this book?

That's a good question and one I wish I had a grand and noble answer for. The truth is, it all started as a good, old-fashioned rant. I simply got annoyed listening to people who really had no idea what they were talking about when it came to AOP, people who were simply spouting forth the same old clichés that they'd heard someone else spout forth — "*… just for writing tests … spaghetti code … patching … blah blah.*"

Whether they were anti-AOP or actually happy users, the majority of them simply had no idea what it was about. I thought a 10-page application note would help clarify some things. "It will take me a couple of days," I foolishly thought. After all, AOP has so few keywords and concepts that it barely qualifies as a methodology.

I failed with the 10-page target. It didn't take me long to discover three important facts:

- A few keywords and concepts can go a long way and have a big impact.

- AOP for verification is not the same as AOP for the rest of the software world.

- No one really knows what an aspect is, or if they do, they can't explain it.

Have a quick search online for AOP or a browse through the increasing number of books on the subject, and you'll probably come away with *absolutely no idea* why this is something you should care about if you're writing verification environments. It's hard to find any examples of the methodology that don't revolve around AspectJ (the AOP version of Java) enterprise software and tell you how it will solve your synchronization, multi-object protocol, persistence, authentication, security, logging, resource pooling, administration, and storage management problems.

Fascinating! I don't recall having any of these in any of the verification environments I've worked on. OK, logging, but who's going to adopt a new methodology just for that? What you will find though, if you dig long enough (or keep reading this book — the choice is yours), is that AOP has another feature that very few people are prepared to discuss, and that's its ability to let you modify code without directly modifying the code. Although there are many good reasons for doing this, it tends to just get called patching and sneered at. This is a very useful feature of AOP, especially for verification environment design.

Why? Well, because life is very different over here in the world of verification. The people are different to start with. Most are not trained and seasoned software engineers — they're hardware engineers writing complex software, possibly for the first time. They are not going to write perfect code, they will not design the ideal class hierarchy or a programming interface that provides the full control needed for any scenario, they are not going to put in all of the hooks and extensibility features needed for a closed solution, and they aren't going to care.

The products are different too. Most of the verification environments written will never be sold, will never be reused in any other projects, and will probably never have to be maintained. OK, we all know the last two are lies, but the project plan says they won't. The schedule says they only have to work *now*.

So, anything that can help create a workable solution quickly, even if it does have a stigma attached, must be considered a valuable tool.

How should I use the book?

I would recommend everyone reads the Introduction. I spent ages working on it, so it will be nice to think it's been read. It sets the scene for the book and explains what I think aspects and AOP are all about. If you have a different view, then the rest of the book might not make that much sense if you skip this part.

What you do after the Introduction will probably depend on how much *e* you know. If you are new to *e* then it's probably worth reading Chapter 2 in detail. If you know *e* already, you can probably get away with just skimming Chapter 2.

Chapters 3 to 6 give some ideas on what you can use aspects for in your verification environment, and how you should go about using them. Everyone should read these chapters. Chapter 7 provides a number of examples of AOP that I find particularly interesting.

Chapter 8 describes a script I wrote that I use to analyze *e* code. I use it a lot when I'm documenting my code or if I'm working with someone else's code. It provides a quick, easy, and free way of working out what you have and where it is. You can get it for free from www.verilab.com.

My top tip

Describing aspects and aspect orientation in a book is one of the more difficult things I've ever tried to do. I think I've succeeded in capturing the essence of it all, but without a white board, hand waving, face-to-face interaction, more hand waving, and a description of how I would use aspects to solve *your* example problem, it's hard to be sure. So I thought I'd start you off with the best advice I have about AOP.

Aspects aren't about language features and keywords — they are a way of thinking about your problems. You don't need an aspect-aware language to start using them. Try this exercise. Print out a program you wrote — C, C++, Perl, etc. — it doesn't matter what. Then decide on a bit of functionality you want to review. It could be the debug logging, some precondition checking, access to a database, help messages, etc. Again, it doesn't matter exactly what you are looking for. Go through your code and circle all the relevant bits with a red pen. Voila — you've isolated your aspect (at least on paper). In an aspect-oriented language, you could have moved all of the circled code somewhere else, physically grouped it so it was encapsulated, and still have it operate exactly where it is on the paper in front of you.

Typographical conventions

> *This book was typeset without the aid of troff, eqn, pic, tbl,*
> *yuc, ick, or any other idiotic Unix acronym.*
>
> The UNIX Haters Handbook [2]

The book was written entirely, and with no problems what-soever, using Word and PowerPoint, partly to annoy those who keep telling me it can't be done. I've used `Courier` to represent code and *`italicized Courier`* to show comments in the code. Commands, such as Specman or Unix commands, are shown using **`bold Courier`**, and program output is shown using **`indented Courier in a slightly smaller font size`**. File names are shown in dark gray. The standard way of communicating visually in OOP is to use the Unified Modeling Language (UML). There have been numerous attempts to extend the UML to deal with AOP as well, but as yet no consensus seems to have been reached. As a result, I have decided to loosely base the diagrams in this book on the UML, but make modifications where I thought it was useful.

Symbols Used in the Book

Symbol	Represents	Comments
Name	A concern	See page 4.
Name	A class	See page 11.
Name	A conceptual aspect	This represents a conceptual aspect (see page 30), and has no reference to the actual implementation of the aspect. For instance, the code in the aspect could be spread across four different files, but a single symbol would be used to represent it. I use the UML's package

		symbol if I need to discuss aspects in terms of implementation structure.
Name	A physical aspect	I'm using the UML symbol for a package to represent a physical aspect (see page 30). This is the actual representation in code of a conceptual aspect.
		When I say package here, I *do not* mean packages defined using the package keyword in *e*, although the concepts might be similar. Instead, a package is simply a grouping of related code. A package can contain other packages, depending on how the code is grouped (directories, files, in-line tags, etc.).
↑	Inheritance	When referring to inheritance in *e* with this symbol, I mean like-inheritance as opposed to when-inheritance.
◆	Composition	The class at the diamond end contains an instance (or a handle to an instance) of the object at the other end.
← <<type>>	A relationship	The classes at either end have a relationship which is specified within the << and >> symbols. The relationship applies in the direction of the arrow. B ← <<creates>> — A This means that class A creates an instance of class B.

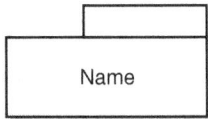

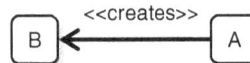

About Verilab

Verilab is an international VLSI engineering consultancy, focusing on the verification and design of complex digital systems. Verilab has helped some of the most advanced VLSI engineering teams in the world improve their capabilities even further. Working at all levels, from verification planning and testbench architecture, through module and system level verification, to entire flow re-engineering, Verilab's expert consultants enable their client teams to achieve tangible, profit-enhancing reductions in design cycle times, increased confidence in the quality of the final device, and lasting ruggedization and reusability in design and verification infrastructure.

1

Introduction to Aspect Oriented Programming (AOP)

A language that doesn't affect the way you think about programming, is not worth knowing.

Alan J. Perlis [4]

If your only exposure to programming technology has been through SystemVerilog or SystemC, you might be forgiven for thinking that object orientation is a brand new idea that's at the cutting edge of software design. After all, the marketing for these languages makes a big deal out of the fact that they are object oriented. While object orientation is a great thing to have in your language, it can hardly be classed as cutting edge. C++, which was released in 1983, drew inspiration from Simula 67 which was about in 1967.

Because object orientation has been around for a while, people have had time to get to know what works and what doesn't. As you'll see from the quotes I've used in the book, people have had enough problems with it to try some new things. Aspect orientation is one of those new things. Although aspect orientation is still classed as new, the first accepted publication using the name was in 1997[1] [5] and the concepts have been around since at least 1978 [6].

---

[1] *e* was around in 1992, which you'll notice is 5 years before AOP was officially developed. The creators of *e* drew their inspiration from many novel programming techniques that were being developed at the time, such as subject oriented

Text continued on next page bottom

In its originally published form [5], aspect orientation is simply an additional way of structuring and encapsulating software. It's normally used in conjunction with object orientation to let you encapsulate a problem's aspects, as well as its structure. I'll explain what an aspect is later, but for now, this simply makes it easier to write code. It isn't very exciting though, unless you are seriously into writing reusable software. This is what most of the mainstream literature focuses on.

Although not part of the original motivation, there is another use of aspect orientation that makes it much more interesting. It's the ability to cleanly add new features to the code without having to intrusively modify the code base. It doesn't sound like much, but it can be a life saver when deadlines loom. Depending on what's going through your mind when you're doing it, it can either be a shameful act (patching) or a wonderfully modern approach to building flexible designs (modular use-case driven development [6]). The boundaries between the shame of patching and the glory of modular use cases are pretty vague and probably not worth getting too concerned about.

So what is an aspect? That's a good question, and one with a rather hard-to-explain answer.

1.1   What are aspects? — Part I

Remember that AO is primarily a mindset.

Markus Völter [9]

In one respect an aspect is like a class — it can be quite difficult to describe exactly what it is. Sure, you can tell people how

---

programming and adaptive programming [7]. So did the developers of AOP [6]. AOP went on to become the most popular of the various approaches; hence, *e* being labeled aspect oriented.

a class is a grouping of related variables and functions and that it's a template for an object which has state, behavior, and identity. You can then go on to talk about inheritance, encapsulation, and polymorphism, but to get across the *essence* of a class, you tend to end up hand waving at a whiteboard, using endless examples that are perfectly obvious to those who know about classes, but a mystery to those who don't.

Aspects make classes look easy. The problem is that an aspect is more abstract and less concrete than a class, so you need to do more hand waving. To start with, at least in *e*, there is no aspect keyword, so straight away you're trying to describe something that doesn't really exist, at least not in a "look, it's the bit after the word 'aspect'" kind of way.

I'm going to use the following example to introduce you to the concepts involved in aspect orientation. It's a very simple example and has absolutely nothing to do with *e*, verification environments, or aspect or object oriented programming. Figure 1.1 shows the topology of a basic design. It is composed of components, such as a CPU, a DMA, a secure digital input output (SDIO) peripheral, and a local memory unit (LMU), and these are connected together by a bus.

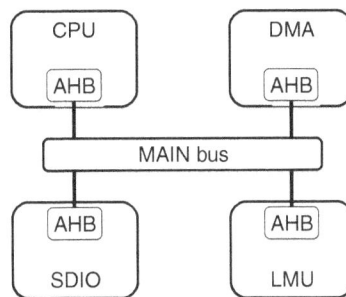

Figure 1.1   The basic design.

Although this is a trivial example, it already shows many features relevant to aspect oriented programming (AOP), even if it isn't coded using aspects. Let's start with a loose definition.

A *concern* is something in the design that you are concerned about. It is something you are interested in, and would probably like to encapsulate to make it reusable or to make it easy to review or replace. The most obvious concerns in the example are the components. Each component is a concern because you would typically want to be able to isolate it from the others so you can reuse it, assign it to one person to design, have it all together in one place for review, and so on. In Verilog, each component would be encapsulated as a module. In VHDL it would be an entity and in SystemC it would be a class.

The bus is also a concern. Why? Because it is something you want to encapsulate and deal with on its own. However, there is something special about this concern, something that makes it different from the individual component concerns. The difference is that it doesn't exist on its own. Instead, it physically cuts across (or interacts with) other concerns. Because of this, it's known as a *crosscutting concern*. In this example it cuts across four other concerns — the CPU, SDIO, DMA, and LMU (Figure 1.2). In order to work with the bus, interface code has to be physically added to these components.

In Figure 1.2, the outer boxes represent the container (module, entity, or class) used to encapsulate the component concerns. The inner boxes represent the code that implements the appropriate concerns. You'll see that whereas the code for the component functionality is fully

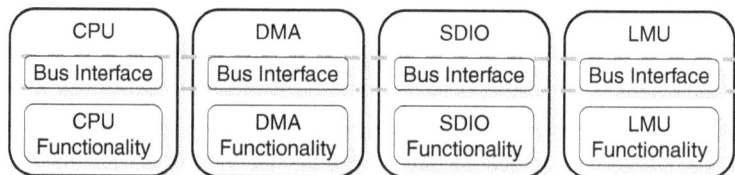

CPU	DMA	SDIO	LMU
Bus Interface	Bus Interface	Bus Interface	Bus Interface
CPU Functionality	DMA Functionality	SDIO Functionality	LMU Functionality

Figure 1.2   The bus crosscutting concern.

contained within the container, the code for the bus interface concern is in all four containers. It cuts across the component concerns.

Now a common argument here is,

> *but I can encapsulate the bus interface easily. I'll just need to create a bus interface class, design a generic interface to the bus, and use a combination of the strategy pattern and the factory pattern to make sure the correct type of bus is instantiated. Simple.*

Sorry, but that won't solve the problem, and Figure 1.3 shows why.

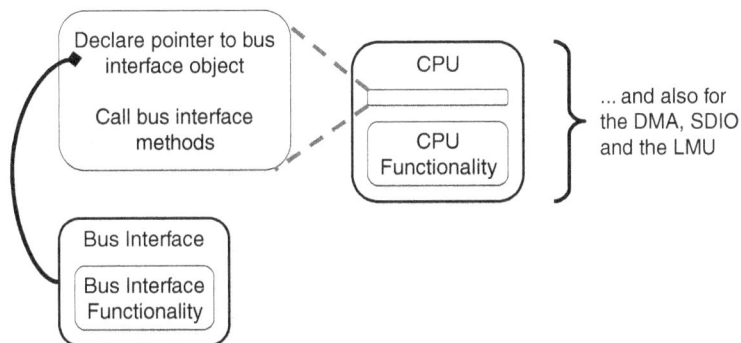

Figure 1.3   An attempt to encapsulate the bus interface crosscutting concern.

In this example, I've created a bus interface container (module, entity, class, etc.) and encapsulated the bus interface code within it. Well, I've encapsulated as much code as I could. The problem is this — to use the code, I still have to have *something* in the CPU, DMA, SDIO, and LMU containers that deals with the bus interface. Sure, it might be a very small amount of code, such as an object instantiation and some interface code, but, and this is vitally important, there is still *some* bus interface code in all of the other concerns.[2] There's no real escaping it, and that can be a problem.

This is so important that I want to make the point again. There is no way in object oriented programming (OOP) to *fully* encapsulate a crosscutting concern. Your dominant concern has to instantiate it, and your dominant concern has to interact with it. By having some of a crosscutting concern in your dominant concerns, no matter how well encapsulated the crosscutting concern may be, your dominant concern now has to care about it. In an ideal world, your dominant concern could ignore it completely.

They don't seem like much, but crosscutting concerns are at the heart of AOP and are the reason why the entire methodology was created. Crosscutting concerns cannot be encapsulated just using object orientation, and that causes problems.

So if crosscutting concerns cause problems, is there anything we can do about them? Yes, there is, and that's where aspect oriented languages come in. They provide language constructs that let you encapsulate crosscutting concerns. Non-crosscutting concerns are coded using OOP techniques as before, and new language constructs are used to code the crosscutting concerns and integrate them with the non-crosscutting concerns. That's right, *"non-crosscutting concerns are coded using OOP techniques as before."* So

---

[2] A perfectly valid argument here is that the CPU, DMA, etc., will always have some form of bus interface, so what does it matter if these classes contain code to deal with it? That's true, but you still have to define some generic interface to all buses, and that's hard to do if you want to take advantage of a particular protocol's interesting features, such as split responses, posted, or out of order writes. Anything you don't include in the interface will preclude the end user making use of that feature.

What it also means is that the designer, who should be entirely focussed on creating a DMA, now has to focus on creating a generic and error-free bus interface in addition to creating the DMA.

straight away all of the OOP experts can relax. OOP's not being thrown away. It's simply being augmented to make it work a bit better.

For now, just assume that an aspect and crosscutting concern are the same thing. An aspect is actually more than this, but that can wait until later (until page 27, to be exact). I'd like to finish off the example to show that you can use aspects without an aspect oriented programming language.[3] If this example design is to be turned into silicon, then it needs to have a clock tree and scan chains added. These are also crosscutting concerns (Figure 1.4).

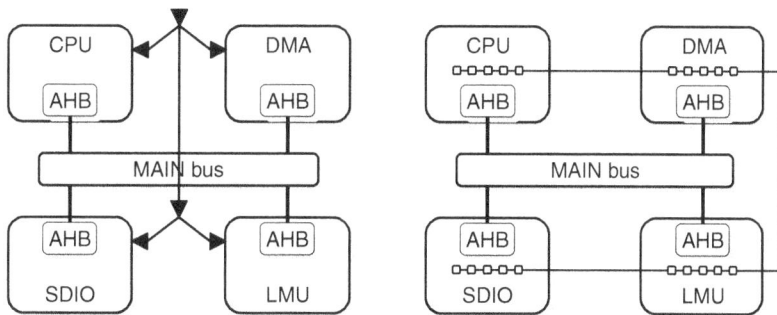

Figure 1.4   The clock tree and scan chain concerns cutting across the component concerns.

Because they are crosscutting concerns, the code that implements the components must be physically modified to contain the code required to implement the clock tree and scan chains (Figure 1.5).

---

[3] My favorite definition of AOP is that aspects are a state of mind. Why? Because aspects are really just a way of thinking about the functionality in your code. You don't actually need language support to think in aspects, which e demonstrates admirably by not having an aspect keyword. Aspect oriented languages do have some language features to help implement aspects, but you can do a lot of it with OOP design patterns if you are *really* keen [9].

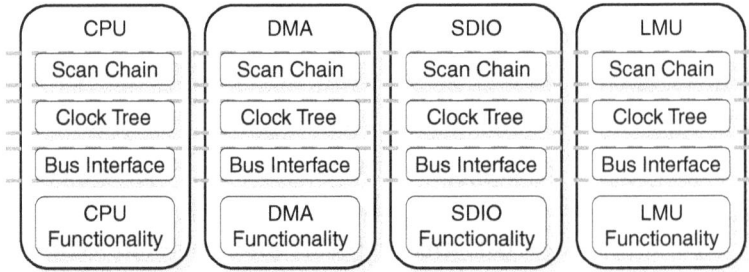

Figure 1.5   The code structure with all concerns.

However, if you open up the source code for any component in an ASIC design, you'll rarely see any clock trees or scan chains. Why? Because these are automatically dealt with using software tools. Information about the clock and scan requirements are encapsulated elsewhere and the required code is

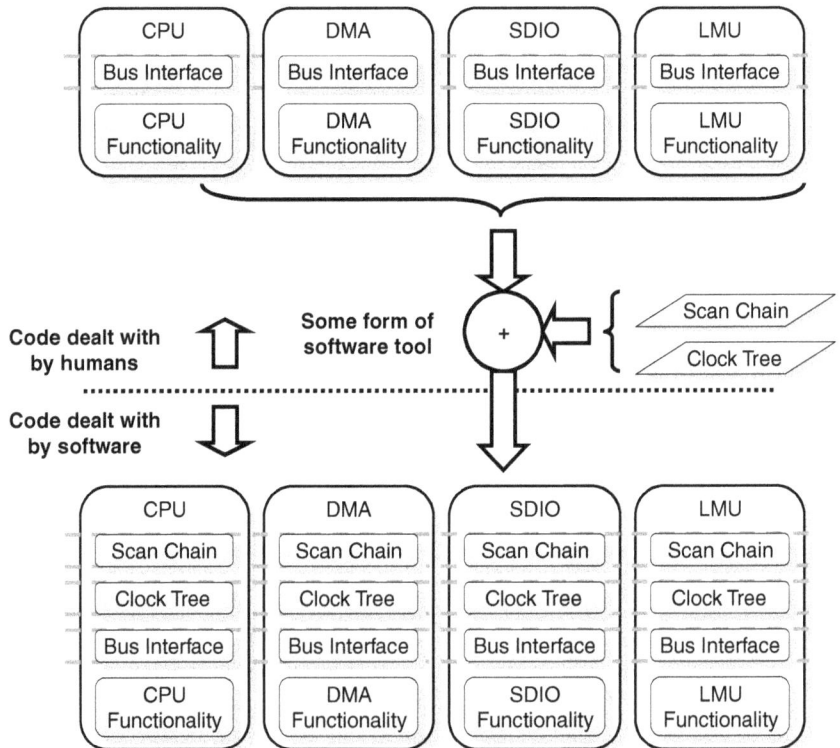

Figure 1.6   Handling aspects in an HDL.

automatically woven in with the component's code. This is aspect oriented programming, which isn't directly supported by Verilog, VHDL, or SystemC (Figure 1.6).

1.2   Why do I need aspects? What's wrong with crosscutting concerns?

If you could do Java over again, what would you change?
I'd leave out classes.

James Gosling, inventor of Java (quoted in [11])

Let's return to our example to show why crosscutting concerns are a problem. Rather than look at the topology of the design, let's look at the code that the designers have to deal with. I'm including the clock tree and scan chain concerns in the components' code because I'm trying to show the problems you'll have if you don't use aspects.

Code that has unencapsulated crosscutting concerns, like in Figure 1.7, has two undesired features. *Code scattering* is where the code for a particular concern appears in multiple places in the design, and *code tangling is* where the code for

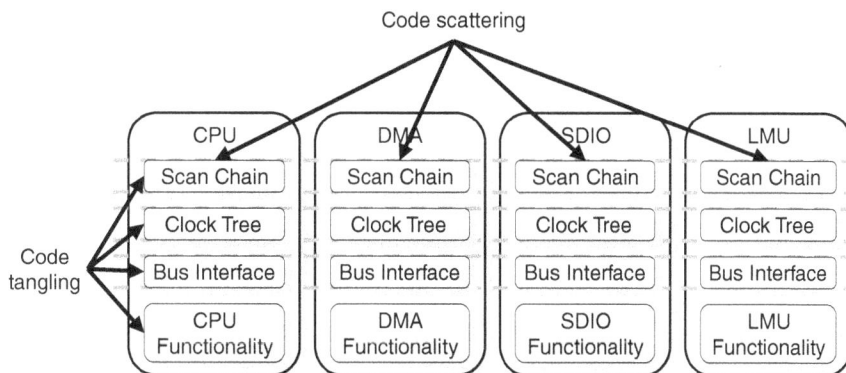

Figure 1.7   The code scattering and code tangling in Figure 1.5.

multiple concerns is tangled together, forcing an object to deal with multiple concerns simultaneously.

The code for the bus interface is scattered across all of the components, as is the code for the clock tree and the scan chains. If you just concentrate on the CPU, you'll see that, apart from the code required to implement the CPU functionality, it also contains the code required to implement the bus interface, the clock tree, and the scan chains.

Code scattering and tangling might appear innocuous, but they can cause a wide variety of problems:

- Code cannot be reused because it contains part of a crosscutting concern that doesn't exist in the new target:
  - None of the components in the example can be used in an FPGA design because of the scan chains and clock trees.
  - None of the components can be used on a non-AHB bus.

- It can be hard to maintain the code:
  - Any changes to the bus interface will require code updates in multiple places.
  - The tangled code obscures the core functionality of a component, so it's hard to focus on the essential code.

- It can be easy to introduce bugs:
  - It's hard to ensure that all scattered code is written consistently.
  - It's hard to ensure that all instances of scattered code are updated if a new feature is added.
  - Without an owner for each crosscutting concern, it's possible that it isn't implemented in all of the places it should be.
  - The designer has to deal with the crosscutting concerns while trying to write the functionality of the non-crosscutting concern.

Aspects let you encapsulate crosscutting concerns, so these problems can be made to go away.

1.3 Surely OOP doesn't have any problems?

Most OOP ideas were alive and well 20 to 25 years ago. Why didn't they solve the software problem then?

Stephen C. Johnson [12]

I mentioned earlier that crosscutting concerns are a problem. You might be thinking that they aren't a problem for you because you use OOP to write your verification environments, and that's state of the art, isn't it?

Well, no, it's not. OOP is old technology, and AOP grew out of a realization that OOP is not as perfect as people seem to think. OOP has been used on projects for a long time now, and many practitioners started to realize quite early on that something was wrong. Even when a problem was mapped to classes, programmers still had to concentrate on many different things at once, software maintenance didn't become trivial, and simple and widespread class reuse remained elusive [13].

The root cause of these problems is that OOP doesn't allow you to decompose a problem into *all* of its concerns. You can only encapsulate some of the concerns. It doesn't easily allow you to deal with crosscutting concerns.

The only structure supported by OOP for encapsulation is the class.[4] When mapping a problem to classes, you have to decide which concerns are the most important and turn them

---

[4] *e* doesn't have a *class* type. Instead, it has structs and units, which, from a software point of view, are classes. There are differences between them, such as when they can be created, whether or not they can control objections, if they can have hdl_paths, etc., but these are unimportant for this book, so I will refer to both units and structs as classes.

into classes. This gives you the structure of your verification environment code. The concerns that you pick to encapsulate in classes are called *dominant concerns*, and these should be independent of each other. Therefore, you could pick CPU and DMA to be dominant concerns because these can be fully encapsulated without knowledge of each other, but you shouldn't pick CPU and monitoring because these are cross-cutting (Figure 1.8). There is no way to encapsulate these in OOP so that they don't have any knowledge of each other. The CPU dominant concern must contain information about monitoring, and the monitoring concern must contain information about CPU. This is poor encapsulation.

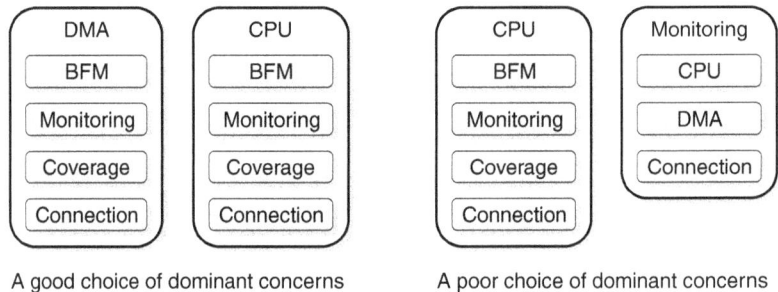

A good choice of dominant concerns   A poor choice of dominant concerns

Figure 1.8   Good and bad choices of dominant concerns.

The remaining crosscutting concerns have to fend for themselves. There is no way to fully encapsulate them in OOP. You could try to create a class to encapsulate a crosscutting concern, such as functional coverage, but you won't succeed. Although you could encapsulate most of it, any concerns that it cuts across still need to instantiate this new class and interact with it in the correct manner. This means there is still some unencapsulated code for the crosscutting concern.

In this example the other classes still need to know that there is functional coverage, and they need to instantiate the functional coverage class and to interact with it. The code required to do this is unencapsulated code. It is nothing to do with the dominant concerns, yet it appears in their code. We couldn't take the dominant concern classes to a new project without taking the functional coverage class with them, and there isn't one place we can go to review all of the functional coverage in the verification environment.

So, if OOP will only let you encapsulate dominant concerns, what should you make the dominant concerns? Perhaps if you make the correct choice then all of the problems will go away?

Let's look at the verification environment code required to verify the SDIO component from the example. The SDIO is a serial transmitter and receiver that supports three different protocols — SD-N (one bit), SD-W (four bits), and SPI. I'll ignore the clock tree and scan chains because they don't exist during functional verification. I'll also ignore the bus interface, because I want to concentrate on the protocols themselves. So what are the dominant concerns?

Dominant concerns should be orthogonal and you would not normally consider the entire verification environment to be a concern. This rules out creating one large class that does *everything* to do with SDIO (Figure 1.9).

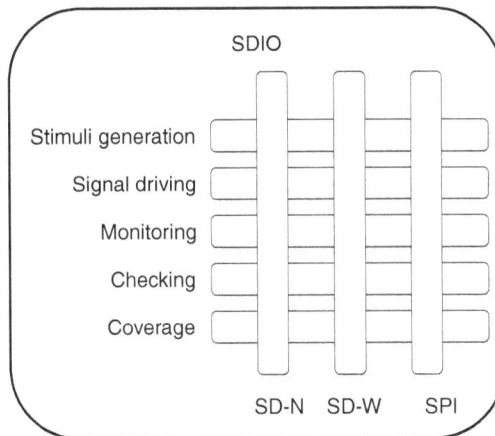

Figure 1.9   Using the SDIO verification environment as the dominant concern.

You could pick the protocols themselves as the thing you want to encapsulate and design a single class that encapsulated everything to do with verifying, say, the SD-N protocol (Figure 1.10).

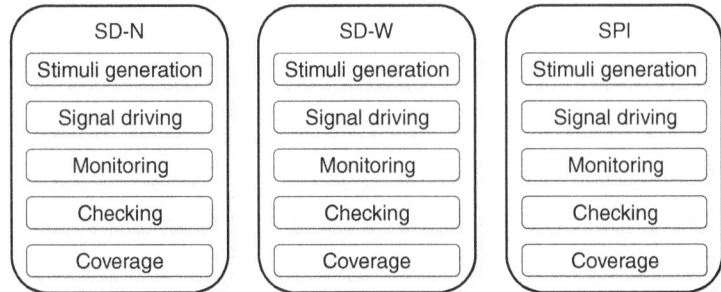

SD-N	SD-W	SPI
Stimuli generation	Stimuli generation	Stimuli generation
Signal driving	Signal driving	Signal driving
Monitoring	Monitoring	Monitoring
Checking	Checking	Checking
Coverage	Coverage	Coverage

Figure 1.10 Structuring your code when protocol is the dominant concern.

But there's a problem with this. For one class to encapsulate everything about the SD-N protocol, then that class would have to generate the stimuli, drive the signals, monitor the signals, check the behavior, and record the functional coverage, and therein lies the problem — programmers intuition, common sense, the entrails, and the e Reuse Methodology (eRM) tell you that you should have individual classes for these. It just feels like a more natural way to do it, probably because these tasks are orthogonal and appear as valid candidates for dominant concerns in their own right.

If you code this way, then you find that the SD-N protocol code is now smeared across several classes (Figure 1.11). There is some in the bus functional model (BFM), there is some in the monitor, and there is some in the checker. The problem now is that the SD-N protocol is no longer encapsulated.

In reality, you would compromise with this approach and create stimuli generators, monitors, signal drivers, checkers, and coverage objects for each of the protocols. This will allow you

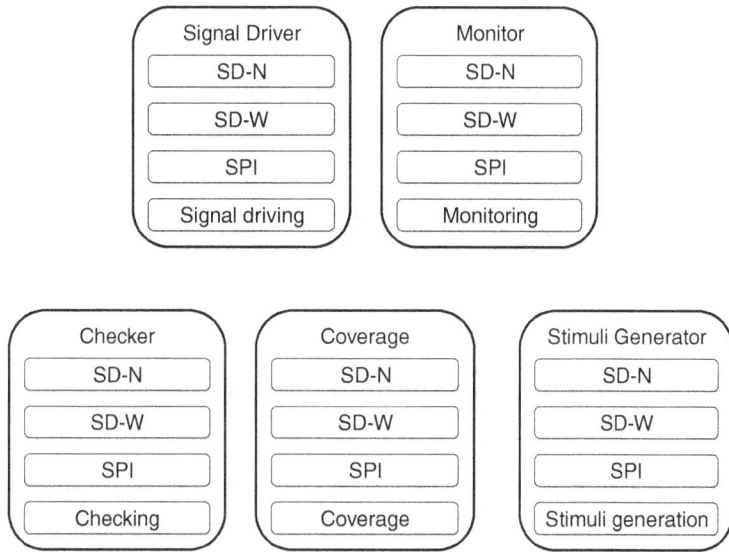

Figure 1.11   Structuring your code when verification environment components are the dominant concern.

to do some encapsulation of the protocols and of the verification environment components. However, this results in poor encapsulation of everything (Figure 1.12). Not only are the protocols unencapsulated, but so are the verification environment components. There is no longer one class that encapsulates everything about, say, the monitoring.[5]

This seems like an acceptable solution, but let's look at what happens if you start taking other concerns into consideration. For instance, the way you connect your verification environment to the device under test (DUT) can be a concern, and we haven't considered that at all. Let's say in your project you want to ensure that all signal maps are implemented using ports

------

[5] You may think that there's no need to encapsulate all monitors in the testbench, but that's probably because it's never really been plausible to do this without AOP. Now that it is a plausible thing to do, you might see some benefit to it. For instance, all monitors can be easily isolated and reviewed to check performance or logging.

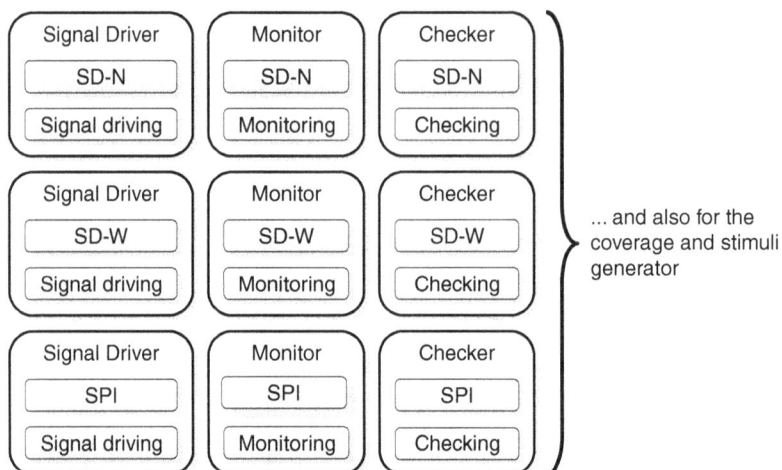

Figure 1.12 A compromise for when verification environment components are the dominant concern.

and that all signals are accessed using methods to deal with some programmable polarities your design has. Your signal drivers and monitors all contain signal connection code, and you have one each of these for each protocol. In the preceding example, your signal connect code would be spread across six different classes. Perhaps if you throw away the structure we already have and make signal connection a dominant concern, then your encapsulation will improve?

Figure 1.13 shows a class structure that would provide ideal encapsulation of your signal connections. This really isn't any better than before. Again, a more pragmatic approach would normally be taken and multiple signal connect classes would be created — one per protocol or one per monitor-and-checker per protocol.

I think it's fair to say that there is no "good" set of dominant concerns in this example that allows everything to be fully encapsulated. No matter what concerns you pick as your dominant concerns, the others become badly encapsulated. This is known as *the tyranny of dominant decomposition* [14].

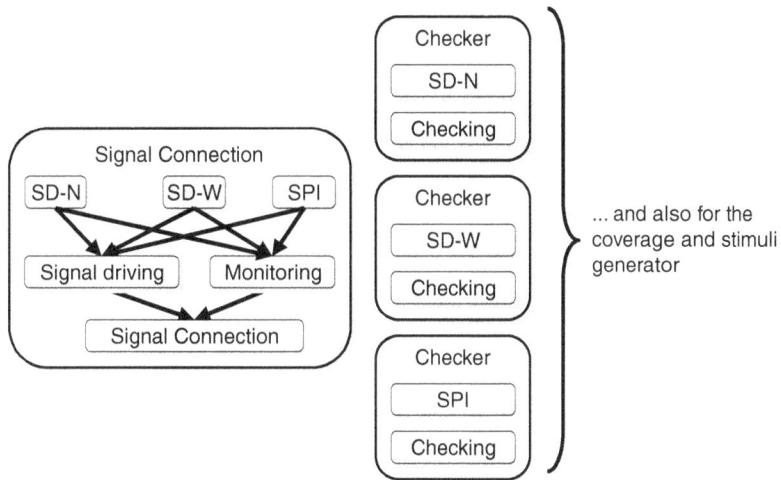

Figure 1.13 The ideal encapsulation of signal connections.

Figure 1.14 shows the signal driver and the monitor classes for the best, and most common, compromise I spoke about earlier. Notice that even when you make the best decisions you can about what the dominant concerns should be and how you structure your code, scattering and tangling still occur.

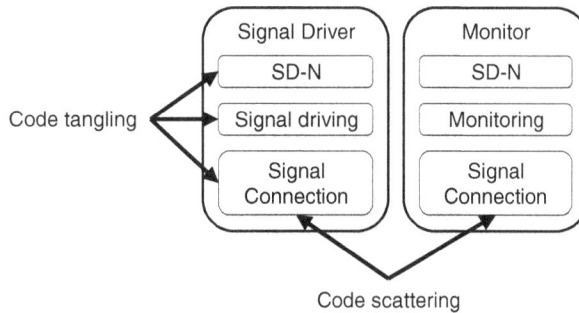

Figure 1.14 The encapsulation of the SD-N protocol.

Many OOP practitioners are unaware of these problems because they are so used to working around them. An argument sometimes used here is that "design patterns solve these problems." They don't. Design patterns are simply proven solutions to common problems, and in general, the problems they are tackling are not code scattering and code tangling. If class A uses a design pattern, you have to modify class A so that it can interact with the design pattern. If class A is part of a design pattern, for example, the observer pattern, then you will have to modify class A's inheritance tree so that it is derived from the correct base class. Just using design patterns can cause scattering and tangling, not eliminate them.

1.4   Why does AOP help?

We can send a message around the world seven times in one second, but it still takes 20 years for that message to go through a quarter inch of human skull.

Stephen C. Johnson [12]

Chapters 3, 4, 5, and 6 of this book go into a lot of detail about how AOP can be used to solve the crosscutting concern problem (and some others as well), but it is probably a good idea to explain here *why* AOP solves the problems that OOP has.

To recap, the problem with OOP is that it can only properly encapsulate one concern in a class. All other concerns have to be scattered throughout the verification environment and tangled with the other code. The class may contain bits of other concerns, but only a dominant concern will exist *fully* within it.

There are only two things that you need to add to an OOP language to turn it into an AOP language. You need the ability to add new members[6] to a class from files other than the one that declared the class, and you need the ability to add functionality to existing class members. These are known *as introduction* and *advice,* respectively.

---

[6]A *member*, or class member, is a property or a method in a class. It's used to describe something that belongs to a class.

And that's it! That's all the extra stuff that an AOP language needs to support aspect orientation. That doesn't seem like much to base a new programming paradigm on, so why does it help? Let's take introductions first. In most (if not all) OOP languages, a class or class header must be defined in a single file. All of the properties and methods that a class needs must be declared in one file, and that leads to code tangling. If you need a property or a method to support a crosscutting concern, it has to be hardwired into the same file that declares all of the properties and methods needed by the dominant concern. Of course, this also leads to code scattering, because you'll need to put the same methods and properties into the definitions of all of the other classes that interact with the crosscutting concern.

However, if you can declare the class and then add new properties and members from other files, you can physically separate the crosscutting concerns from the dominant concern.

Well, almost. You can physically separate the properties and methods needed for the various concerns, but you still have to deal with the *use* of these properties and methods. That's where advice comes in. Advice lets you alter the functionality of an existing class by adding new functionality at *join points*, which are simply well-defined points in the code. Method calls are the most common joint point, but *e* supports some others, such as coverage groups, coverage items, and events.[7] For method advice (I'll talk about the others later), you can say "execute advice A before method M," "execute advice A after method M," or "execute advice A instead of method M."

---

[7] Defining these as join points stretches the commonly understood definition a bit because coverage groups, coverage items, and events aren't part of the program's flow of execution. However, advice is really a behavior modifier, and you can statically alter the behavior of coverage groups, coverage items, and events in *e*.

Why does this help? Well, you can now build up the behavior of a method from several places. In the class definition that deals with the dominant concern, you can just deal with the dominant concern. In the files that deal with the crosscutting concerns, you can now hook in the necessary behavior, assuming you have a join point at the right place.[8]

So, AOP is simply this: it's a way of structuring your code that lets you build a class up in individual pieces, or slices of functionality.

Figure 1.15 shows the scattering and tangling problem for a subset of the example in Figure 1.7. On the left are the concerns — the functional areas that the verification environment has to deal with. In this example, the concerns we are

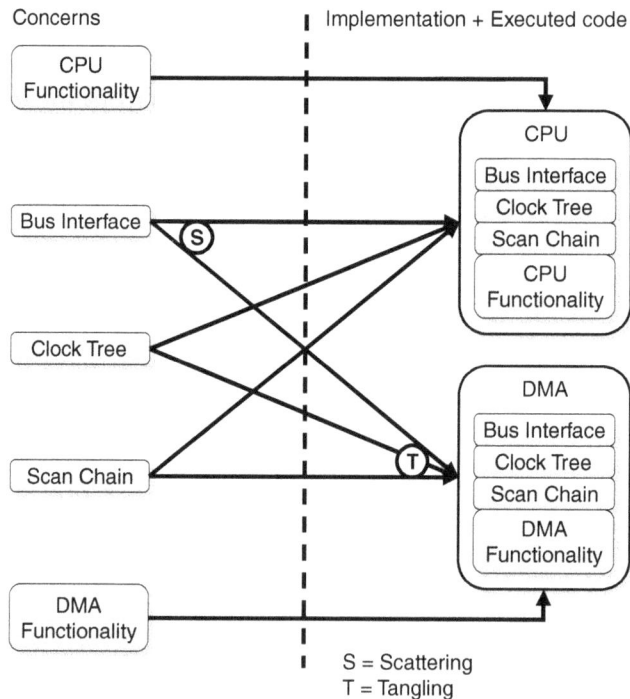

Figure 1.15   The scattering and tangling problem.

---

[8] This means you'll want to write your code using as many methods as you can. This is now generally accepted [16] as good practice even without AOP.

interested in are the CPU and DMA core functionality, along with the bus interfaces, the clock tree, and the scan chains.

On the right are the classes that exist within the design. These are the classes you edit and they are the classes that get executed. As the only place code can be encapsulated is in these classes, code for the clock tree appears scattered in two classes, and in each class it is tangled with some other code (scan chain, bus interfaces, etc.). This is shown by the concerns embedded inside the classes. If you were to open up the file for one of these classes, you would see scan chain code, clock tree code, bus interface code, and core functionality code.

Figure 1.16 shows how aspects remove the scattering and tangling problems. In the middle of the diagram are aspects and classes. Each class contains the class definition and the core functionality encapsulated by the class, but nothing else. In

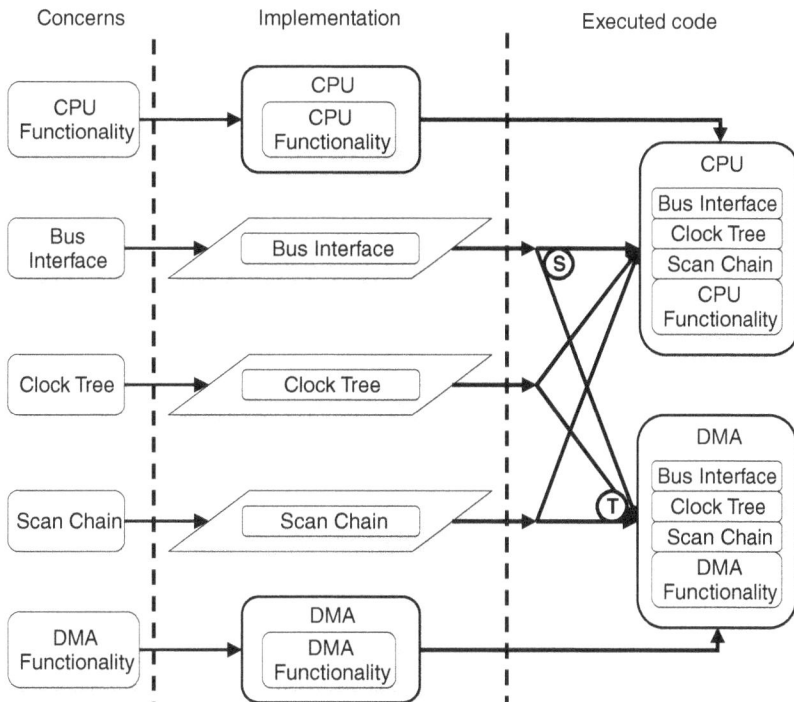

Figure 1.16   How aspects remove the scattering and tangling problem.

particular, they contain nothing to do with clock trees, bus interfaces, or scan chains. Each aspect extends these classes to add the advice and introductions necessary to deal with a particular crosscutting concern, such as clock tree or scan chain.

Note that there is no scattering or tangling of code *within* the aspects. If we want to see *everything* to do with clock trees, we open up the clock tree aspect.

Of course, this changes after the weaving stage,[9] and the code is as tangled and scattered as before. You can see this on the right-hand side of the diagram. However, this is an automatic process as part of the compile step, so you never have to deal with this code directly. In fact, you don't even get to see it. All you deal with are the classes and aspects in the middle of the diagram.

1.5   Theory vs real life — What else is AOP good for?

You have your "isa" hierarchy all thought out — let's say you have a 'mammals' class and a 'reptiles' class and so on — and you start to implement it, and along comes a platypus, a fur-bearing, egg-laying, duck-billed creature, which doesn't appear to fit in any of the classifications you've created.

Talin [15]

The previous section introduced AOP and explained why it was gaining in popularity in the software world. By allowing us to encapsulate crosscutting concerns, we can avoid the

---

[9] The *weaver* is the tool that integrates the aspects with the objects. Conceptually, it acts like a preprocessor that takes the class, physically adds all introductions to the class definition, and inserts the advice code into the join points. In reality, the Specman tool that processes and executes *e* does not have a preprocessing weaver because it can compile most of the *e* code and still apply extensions to it at runtime by loading an interpreted *e* file [7]. This is a technical issue that is fairly unimportant. It helps to imagine it has a weaver. It is a good lie.

code scattering and code tangling problems. At this point it is probably worth noting that there are two types of verification engineers. The first, engineers with an interest in software, are either agreeing wholeheartedly with the preceding discussion about the problems with OOP or claiming that I'm a blasphemous heretic. It's probably best that the latter stop reading now, because it's going to get a lot worse. The second group, hardware engineers struggling to write verification environments, are probably going *"huh?"* or *"so what?"*. This section will try to address this group.

It is important to realize that many verification engineers today are just temporarily rebranded hardware engineers whose turn it is to do some verification. They haven't been trained to write software, they haven't been shown what can be achieved, many are simply not interested in making a proper job of it, and those who try frequently run into schedule problems because there is never enough time allocated to the task. After all, the verification environment is not part of the product! Mainstream verification environment design is unfortunately about solving problems *now*, without any care about how hard you may have made your life tomorrow.

Simply put, many verification environments are being written by people who are effectively unskilled in the job. Just as we wouldn't expect a software engineer to design a multiclock domain ASIC device, why should we expect a hardware engineer to create a medium-sized software program?

As a result of this, many verification environments are being written using poor naming conventions, insufficient commenting, poor object composition, and overuse and misuse of inheritance. They rely far too heavily on public member variables, contain a plethora of hardwired values, and have poor abstraction and encapsulation. Many verification environments simply cannot be kept alive until the end of the project, never mind maintained and reused for derivative and next-generation designs. With such an array of basic problems in verification environments, is it any wonder that discussions about crosscutting concerns are likely to fall on deaf and uncomprehending ears?

Perhaps the biggest advantage AOP has in verification environment design then is not the ability to solve some high-level problems, that are frankly pretty minor compared to the other problems in today's code, but its ability to help verification engineers solve complex problems *now*. Yes, I'm talking about using AOP to patch code. Now once the software puritans reading have stopped choking (and declaring me a blasphemous heretic), we can take time to look at what this actually means. You see, OOP also has some other problems that, although not as conceptual as crosscutting concerns, are practical problems because they can cause you to miss your deadlines. Surely anything that can do this should warrant careful consideration?

If there is one feature that makes people distrust AOP, then it's AOP's ability to patch code. Being able to change the functionality of a class without directly modifying the class source file seems to be abhorrent to some. "You can't read the code and know the functionality," they cry, neatly ignoring the fact that OOP has an *even worse* version of the same problem. When you have a pointer to a base class that has virtual methods, only a *runtime* analysis of the program will tell you what method actually gets called. At least with AOP, only a compile time analysis is needed.[10] As you will see in this book, patching code is simply a pragmatic programming technique that allows verification environment designers to concentrate on finding DUT bugs and not waste time trying to craft the perfect verification environment.

---

[10] If you use conditional AOP, then you also have to do a runtime analysis, but all the information you need to work out what will get called is stored in the class's determinant fields, so it's not really an issue. Yes, I know I haven't defined conditional AOP yet, but the index is your friend.

So why is patching so useful? Well, imagine that you cannot patch code — that all changes made to a class must be made to its source file or through inheritance and polymorphism. Also imagine that the class you are working with, a BFM for a packet-based serial transmitter, has a bug in the `transmit()` method.

There are two options open to you to fix this bug. You can modify the original source code of the `transmit()` method or you can use inheritance to create a new subtype containing your bug fix. Modifying the source code is not always possible:

- It may be commercial code that is encrypted, so you can't change it. You can ask the supplier for a bug fix, but that takes time.

- The code may be referenced from a central repository, where you don't have write access. You can ask the original author to make the changes, but again, this takes time. Changing code in a repository has an impact on all other projects using it, and they will all have to be reregressed. You could try to take a local copy, but your build environment may always reference the repository version.

- The original code may be yours and stored locally. Although you are free to make the changes, you will prevent your verification environment from compiling until it is done. If the bug is complex, this may take several days. In the meantime, you may need to run the verification environment to recreate a DUT bug, which you now can't do.[11]

So, changing the original code may not be possible or desirable. The other option is to use inheritance to create an extended version of the class. The new class just contains a new

---

[11] You can use your revision control software to step back to an old version or to create a branch for your changes, but few people seem to do this.

version of the `transmit()` method with the bug fixed. There are two potential problems here. The first is that you now have a new class type, and the only way your new `transmit()` method will get called is if you create an object of your new type. If the BFM is not yours in the first place, then the chances are high that your code does not instantiate the BFM directly, which means you can't change the instantiation to use your new BFM class. To use your new class will require changes to other source code, which, for the reasons stated previously, may not be possible. In fact, if you can change the code that instantiates the BFM, you can probably change the BFM.

The second possible problem is quite technical. If the BFM is upcast anywhere in the code, i.e., it is accessed through a pointer that has the type of the base class, then the polymorphism will only work if the `transmit()` method in the base class is declared as virtual. If it is not virtual, the original `transmit()` method will continue to get called. It is very common for people not to declare methods as virtual because they are inexperienced and didn't know the impact of this, they are experienced but forgot to type `virtual`, or they are experienced and were deliberately closing off the class to further extensions.

This all means that, in some quite common cases, you will not be able to fix a bug in a class using OOP. With AOP, the situation is very different. Because AOP allows you to change the functionality and structure of a class without having to modify the original code, all of the OOP problems go away. You don't need to have access to the original source code to replace a method with a new version, you don't have to create a new class type, and you don't have to remember to declare the original method in a special way. Encountering a bug like this while using an AOP language is not typically an issue.

The preceding arguments also hold if you want to add new functionality to a class, such as the ability to transmit a new protocol. An OOP language may force you to do some complex refactoring of the code, assuming you can get access to the code. With aspects, adding new functionality is trivial. Aspects therefore have another benefit. Because it is now easy to patch code, verification environment writers only have to write the code that is absolutely necessary at that moment in time. They do not have to write functionality that *may* be useful at a future date [16].

Of course, wanton patching is poor technique, and can lead to very complex code. Once a bug has been fixed or the new functionality added, the original source code should be updated with the changes. However, this can now be done at a suitable time of your choosing.

1.6   What are aspects? — Part II

The definition I gave earlier of an aspect being a crosscutting concern is good, but it could be better. It seems like the most complex part of AOP is coming up with an exact definition for an aspect. This is not helped by the fact that the word "aspect" is used for two different meanings. In OOP, a "class" is the physical representation of a "dominant concern." In AOP, an aspect is the physical representation of an aspect. This isn't helpful.

Without an aspect keyword, e makes it hard to define the physical meaning of an aspect. To simplify things, let's assume for now that whatever we decide a "conceptual aspect" to be, a "physical aspect" is just the code representing an encapsulated version of it. A fuller definition can be found on page 30.

A common definition of an aspect is that it is a well-modularized crosscutting concern [5]. This definition of an aspect describes what it conceptually is, but gives no aid in mapping the concept to actual code. Some other definitions offer more practical advice. Webopedia [18] uses the following definition:

> *Aspects in aspect-oriented programming (AOP) package advice and pointcuts into functional units in much the same way that object-oriented programming uses classes to package fields and methods.*

In *e* this would be advice and introduction, because pointcuts[12] don't really exist in *e*.

I find this all a bit intangible though, so I prefer to start with another definition of aspect, where it is a use case or horizontal slice of functionality in the design [6]. The horizontal concept comes from assuming that your dominant concerns (classes) are vertical, and the aspects are stacked on top of them. Figure 1.5 shows what I mean by this. This helps me visualize the program, a verification environment in our case, as a series of interwoven slices of functionality that can be added, removed, and replaced without having to modify any code that isn't in the aspect.

But that isn't quite what I mean when I talk about aspects either. I like to stretch the concept a bit further. The problem I have with an aspect being a horizontal slice of functionality is this — what happens when some code belongs to multiple slices of horizontal functionality? Do we not then end up with the same problems as before, that the code is scattered across different aspects? As an example, let's look at two use cases for a DMA controller:

■ Configuring a transfer: The software writes to the DMA controller's configuration registers to set up a transfer;

---

[12] A *pointcut* is list of join points that a particular piece of advice can be applied to. In *e*, a particular piece of advice can only be applied to one join point, so pointcuts aren't needed.

■ Clearing an interrupt: The software writes to the DMA controller's interrupt register to clear an interrupt.

Both of these require a slave bus interface, so which use case (or horizontal slice) does this belong to?

So, I don't define aspects to be a "horizontal slice" of functionality. I define them to be a "slice" of functionality. I don't care which direction they're going in. This might sound a bit picky, but it does have a big effect because it lets you assign code to multiple aspects, it lets you treat multiple aspects as one aspect, and it lets you treat a concern as an aspect, not just a crosscutting concern. It also lets you use the word aspect as it is defined in the dictionary — as a feature, facet, or a way in which something can be viewed by the mind.

A good way to visualize this is to imagine that your code is stored in a large database that you can query. You can ask the database to return just the code that deals with feature X, or where features X and Y interact, and it will do so.

Let's go back to the example in Figure 1.1 (page 3). Imagine all of the code that defined this design, including the clock trees and scan chains, was stored in this database. What kind of queries could I make? What aspects are there to this design? Here are some examples:

Query	Returned code
Show me all the code for the CPU's core functionality	All the code for the CPU, but excluding the bus interface, scan chain, and clock tree
Show me the code I've patched into the SDIO to temporarily fix the transmit bug	The code in this particular patch
Show me all the code where the CPU interacts with the AHB bus interface	The code where the bus interface interacts with the CPU
Show me all the code for the scan chains in the LMU and SDIO	The code where the scan chains interact with the LMU and the SDIO

The last two queries are examples of how an aspect can be made up of other aspects. The preceding queries deal with functional concerns, but I can define structure as a concern as well. I could say that I wanted to see all the code that dealt with CPU and monitoring, and what do I get? I get the CPU Monitor class!

So, that's my definition of an *aspect* —it is a particular view of your code. The query is a *conceptual aspect,* and the code returned is the *physical aspect.* The trick now is how to structure your code to make this happen. Without such a database, you'll have to organize your code so that you can isolate aspects. That means you'll have to manually define the aspects you are interested in, normally when you start writing the code. If the code for an aspect is scattered throughout the code base and cannot be isolated in some manner, then I don't consider it an aspect, just a mess. Remember that the original definition contained the words "well modularized."

There are several techniques for structuring your code, such as tagging the code (see "8.12. Finding aspects" on page 231), storing all the code for an aspect in a single file, spreading the code across several specially named files (see 3.3. "Mapping aspects to files" on page 75), and storing all the code in a particular directory, etc. In this book, all files that combine to make up an aspect are referred to as *aspect files.*

So well done for making it this far. You now know just about all you need to know about the theory of AOP. The rest of the book delves into technical details about how to use AOP in e (Chapter 2) and explains what you can use it for and the advantages it can bring (Chapters 3 to 6). Some examples of AOP in action, based on real project experience, are given in Chapter 7. Chapter 8, "Analyzing e Code," is completely optional, but worth reading.

2
AOP in *e*

Frankly, they are wrong, and I don't have very much patience for people who get religious about tools and judge things that they haven't used.

Joel Spolsky [16]

In this chapter I'm going to take you through AOP as it is implemented in *e*. When you do your search for AOP on the Internet or browse the books in your local bookshop, you'll almost inevitably start reading about AspectJ, and you'll notice that none of it seems to be particularly relevant to verification environment design. Example crosscutting concerns such as synchronization, persistence, shared resource access, authentication, and security problems just don't seem to map too well to verification environments.

Depending on your existing *e* knowledge, you may also notice one other important point:

*It's not quite the same AOP as **e** supports.*

AspectJ supports more types of join points than *e*, and advice can be applied to multiple join points from one statement (using pointcuts), but *e* has *conditional AOP*, which is a way of specifying that certain advice and introductions only apply when the class meets certain runtime conditions. So, rather than explain all of the concepts in AOP, I'll limit this discussion to the subset actually supported by *e*.

In the Introduction I defined two new concepts that make up AOP: introduction and advice. I'm going to go over these again in more detail, describing how they are applied in *e*. I'm also going to describe extension, which is the mechanism *e* uses to add advice and introductions to a class.

Now you might assume that all of this stuff here is covered in the Specman help file, and you'd be right. It's in there. Somewhere. Finding it though, and understanding how to use it is not always easy. Understanding the implications of what it says can be difficult. Anyone who has used *e* for more than a few weeks will probably know about all of the *concepts* mentioned here, but there are a few subtle points that you might not know about.

I am using this chapter to take you through the language features that I consider the most important. I'm not attempting to cover all language features related to AOP, because they are not all equally important. If I haven't discussed it here, it's because I've never found a need to use it on a project. I do however, spend quite a bit of time explaining some of the nonobvious side effects of some of the features. For example, I talk about what really happens when you use when-inheritance and why returning from a method extension can be bad for your verification environment and bad for your sanity.

So even if you know the *e* language syntax, I'd encourage you to at least skim through this chapter looking for the juicy bits that perhaps you don't already know. For those who don't know *e*, this chapter will give you a short and simple introduction to its AOP language features without the overhead of explaining all the nuances.

Introduction

An introduction in AOP is when you add, or introduce, a new property into a class, enumerated type, or cover group. The exact definition of property will depend on the target of the introduction.

Introductions into classes.

When introducing a property into a class, the property can be a method, a field, an event, a constraint definition, or a cover group. The class is extended using the `extend` keyword, and the properties are added as normal.

```
extend my_class{
  new_property: uint;
};
```

Introductions into enumerated types.

When introducing a property into an enumerated type, the property is simply a new value that the type can take on. The introduction is made using the `extend` keyword.

```
extend my_enumerated_type: [new_property];
```

Introductions into cover groups.

When introducing a property into a cover group, the property is simply an item, a cross, or a transition. The introduction is made by extending the cover group using `is also`.

```
extend my_class{
  cover my_coverage_group is also{
    item new_property: int = get_transaction().a;
  };
};
```

Advice

Advice is *e* code that is to be executed at a join point. As there are several types of join points in *e*, I'll take them one at a time.

Method join points.

Three types of advice exist for methods:

■ is first advice gets executed *before* the code at the join point;

■ is also advice gets executed *after* the code at the join point;

■ is only advice gets executed *instead of* the code at the join point.

The code originally at the join point is called the *root method*. The root method plus all of its advice are referred to collectively as the method.

```
extend my_class{
   my_method() is       {}; // The root method
   my_method() is first{}; // is first advice
   my_method() is also{}; // is also advice
   my_method() is only{}; // is only advice
};
```

Event join points.

Advice can be added to events, but only the is only type of advice. That means you can replace the definition of an event, but you can't add to an existing event.

```
extend my_class{
   event my_event is only cycle @clk;
};
```

Cover group and cover item join points.
Advice is added to cover groups and cover items using the
`using also` keywords, which allow you to add new options
to the group or item. You cannot add new cover items to a
group this way.

```
extend my_class{

  // Add advice to a cover group
  //
  cover my_coverage_group using also
    text = "A Proper Name for the Coverage
    Group";

  // Add advice to an existing cover item. The
  // "is also" is needed on the group to give
  // you access to the existing property.
  // Because of this, you can also add a new
  // property while you're here
  //
  cover my_coverage_group is also{
    item existing_property using also radix = HEX;
  };
};
```

Extension

An *extension* modifies a single named class and contains
advice and/or introductions that will modify that class. A
class can have more than one extension, but an extension cannot modify more than one class. This means that multiclass
crosscuts cannot be encapsulated in one extension.

The use of *determinant* fields to limit the scope of the extension is novel to the AOP used in *e* and is key to making AOP
actually useful. A determinant is simply a Boolean or enumerated field that is used to discriminate between different

subtypes of the same class. Without this ability, any extension would be global, which, as I discuss in "2.8. How do I limit the scope of my extensions?" (page 53), is something you sometimes need to avoid. I like to call this feature conditional AOP, because it specifies the runtime conditions that must be satisfied before the introduction and advice are applied to a class.

2.1 How do I extend a class?

PROBLEM   I want to extend a class to introduce a new property or add some advice.

SOLUTION   Before you can add advice or an introduction to a class, you have to extend it first. The syntax for this is:

```
extend <DETERMINANTs> <CLASS NAME>{
};
```

For

```
extend <CLASS NAME>{
when <DETERMINANTs 1> <CLASS NAME>{
  <MEMBER DECLARATION>;
 };
 when <DETERMINANTs n> <CLASS NAME>{
  <MEMBER DECLARATION>;
 };
};
```

■ <DETERMINANTs> represents an optional space delimited string of determinant values. If used, the extensions only apply to classes where the determinants match the specified values.

■ <CLASS NAME> is the name of the class you want to extend.

DISCUSSION   Creating an extension of a class can be done using one or two keywords, depending on the approach you want to take. extend can be used exclusively, or you can choose to use when as well. However, there is no obvious reason to use when in addition to extend. You have to type in the class name more often (once for the class extension and then once again for each when block), the code for the extensions become cluttered, tangled, and scattered, and you lose many of the advantages of separating crosscutting concerns.

Extending a class using determinants is known as *when-inheritance* (whether or not the when keyword is used). This is because it appears to create new subclasses that only appear when the determinants take on the correct values.

Note the word "appear." One point that is very important to understand is that when you make introductions using when-inheritance and the determinants are not declared as const[13], the new members are *not* added to a *new* type of class. They are added to the basic class, but can only be accessed when the determinant fields have the correct values. We can therefore think of when-inheritance as creating a new view onto a class, rather than creating a new type of class. This is important, because every new member you add increases the memory requirements for every instance of the class, whether the determinant fields allow access or not.

For example, be warned if you intend to add a fixed size list with 1 million elements to your class when the packet determinant is VERY_RARE. Even instances of ULTRA_COMMON and REALLY_COMMON packets will get the memory overhead of the list as well.

---

[13] There are some good reasons for not using const determinants though, and I'll cover one of them in the section "7.1. Creating a class with a selectable algorithm." Sometimes it's just helpful to be able to dynamically change the type of a class by changing the determinant value, and const will stop you from doing this.

EXAMPLE   The following code defines a struct to hold information
about a DMA transfer:

```
type dma_transfer_kind_t: [];

struct dma_transfer_s{
  kind: dma_transfer_kind_t;

  // This method is declared as undefined,
  // because each extension of this struct must
  // define a version of this
  //
  how_many_left(): uint is undefined;
};


// Note that the name of a determinant (kind in
// this case) can be omitted if there is only
// one field in the class that can take on the
// value of the determinant (LLP in this case).


// Because it's unlikely that you'll put
// another field of type dma_transfer_kind_t in
// here, omitting 'kind is probably a safe
// thing to do. However, if the determinant
// kind was of type Boolean, then I'd suggest
// always mentioning the determinant's name.
// Adding another Boolean field to a class at a
// later date is likely.
//
extend dma_transfer_kind_t: [LLP];

extend LLP dma_transfer_s{
  // or extend LLP'kind dma_transfer_s{
  // This field keeps track of where the
  // transfer is — which block is being
  // transferred. It can only be accessed
  // when kind == LLP. However, it always
  // consumes memory.
  //
  current_block    : uint;
```

```
  // This field specifies how many blocks are in
  // the transfer. It can only be accessed when
  // kind == LLP. However, it always consumes
  // memory.
  //
  number_of_blocks: uint;

  // This method returns the number of blocks
  // remaining in the transfer. Although the
  // prototype has been defined in the base
  // class, the specific functionality is defined
  // here. When kind == LLP, it is this code
  // that will get called.
  //
  how_many_left(): uint is {
    result = number_of_blocks - current_block;
  };
};

extend dma_transfer_kind_t: [RELOADING];

extend RELOADING dma_transfer_s{

  // This field keeps track of where the
  // transfer is - which reload is being
  // processed. It can only be accessed when
  // kind == RELOADING. However, it always
  // consumes memory.
  //
  current_reload   : uint;

  // This field specifies how many reloads are in
  // the transfer.  It can only be accessed
  // when kind == RELOADING. However, it always
  // consumes memory.
  //
  number_of_reloads: uint;

  // This method returns the number of reloads
  // remaining in the transfer. Although the
  // prototype has been defined in the base
```

```
  // class, the specific functionality is defined
  // here. When kind == RELOADING, it is this
  // code that will get called.
  //
  how_many_left(): uint is {
    result = number_of_reloads - current_reload;
  };
};
```

Code Listing 1. The LLP and RELOADING extensions of the dma_transfer_s class.

Figure 2.1 shows how when-inheritance works for the code in Code Listing 1. The box on the left shows the combined contents of the struct, which has two extensions, one where kind == LLP and one where kind == RELOAD. This is what Specman stores in memory for *every* instance of dma_transaction_s, *irrespective* of the value kind has. The boxes on the right side show you what you can actually access when the kind field takes on its different values. The gray fields with a line through them cannot be accessed in this

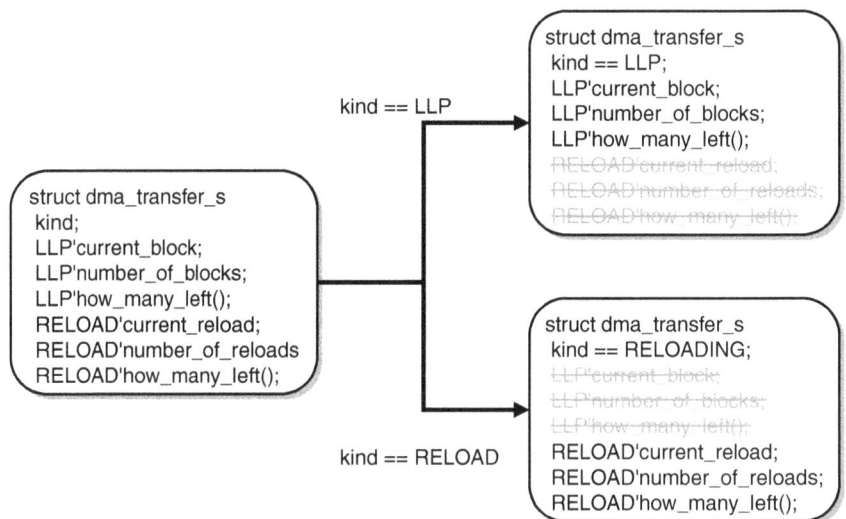

Figure 2.1 How when-inheritance actually works.

view, although they are still present and consume memory. Although these look like different types, they are in fact just different views onto the same type.

2.2 How do I extend a class for multiple values of a determinant?

PROBLEM   I want to make identical extensions to a class for several values of a determinant field. However, the *e* syntax doesn't seem to allow this.

SOLUTION   Create a new Boolean determinant that is true when you want the extensions to be applied and false otherwise.

DISCUSSION You can use multiple determinant fields to control your extensions, but you cannot use multiple values for the *same* determinant field. The syntax of the language simply doesn't allow it. The following is illegal:

```
extend [EVEN, ODD]'parity uart_packet_s{
  // Your introductions and advice for parity go
  // here
};
```

Instead, it looks like you'll have to duplicate your new code:

```
extend EVEN'parity uart_packet_s{
  // Your introductions and advice for parity
  // go here
};
extend ODD'parity uart_packet_s{
  // Your introductions and advice for parity
  // go here
};
```

A better solution is to add a new determinant field that indicates whether you have parity as follows:

```
type parity_type_t is : [NONE, EVEN, ODD];
struct uart_packet_s{
  parity : parity_type_t;
  keep soft parity == NONE;


  // The following field is TRUE when we have
  // some form of parity and FALSE otherwise
  //
  has_parity: bool;
  keep parity in [EVEN, ODD] =>
                        has_parity == TRUE;
  keep parity == NONE        =>
                        has_parity == FALSE;
};


extend TRUE'has_parity uart_packet_s{
  // Your introductions and advice for parity
  // go here
};
```

2.3 How do I extend a type?

PROBLEM   I want to add a new value to an enumerated type. Can I do this?

SOLUTION   Yes you can:

```
extend <TYPE> : [<NEW VALUES>];
```

DISCUSSION   Extending a type is very easy.

■ <TYPE> is the name of the type you want to extend.

■ <NEW VALUES> is a comma separated list of the values
   you want to add.

<small>EXAMPLE</small>

```
type packet_t   : [CONTROL, PAYLOAD];
extend packet_t : [ROUTING];
```

This code adds the value ROUTING to the `packet_t` type, which will now have the following values: CONTROL, PAYLOAD, and ROUTING.

2.4 How do I introduce a new noncoverage member to a class?

<small>PROBLEM</small>   I want to add a new method, field, constraint, or event to an existing class. What do I do?

<small>SOLUTION</small>   Extend the class as described earlier and add your new non-coverage member to the class. The introduction you make uses exactly the same syntax as it would if you were adding it to the class when it is defined.

<small>DISCUSSION</small>   Adding a method, field, or event to a class as part of an extension is called an introduction. Once the class extension has been made, no special syntax is required to actually make the introduction. You just declare your new member as you would normally do. If, through introduction, the class ends up with multiple members (of the same category — method, field, or event) that have the same name, Specman will use the determinant fields at runtime to select which instance of the member should be accessed.

> NOTE: This is not true for coverage groups, which must have unique names in subtypes. See "How do I introduce a coverage group to a class?" on page 44 for more information.

If you are adding a method to multiple subtypes, the methods do not need to have the same prototypes or return values, unless the method has been defined in a base type. In this case, the method prototype in the subtypes must match that in the base type.

EXAMPLE

```
// Use when-inheritance to create a new subtype
// of dma_transfer_s. This subtype will only be
// used when dma_transfer_s.kind equals LLP.
//
extend LLP dma_transfer_s{
  // Introduce a new field
  //
  number_of_blocks : uint;

  // Introduce constraints for the new field.
  // You could easily add constraints for an
  // existing field
  //
  keep soft number_of_blocks > 0;
  keep soft number_of_blocks < 5;

  // Introduce a new method
  //
  how_many_left() : uint is{
   // Code omitted for clarity
  };
};
```

2.5 How do I introduce a coverage group to a class?

PROBLEM

I want to add a new coverage group to an existing class. What do I do?

SOLUTION

Extend the class as described earlier and add your new coverage group to the class. The introduction you make uses exactly the same syntax as it would if you were adding it to the class when it is defined. However, please read the following discussion on the naming restrictions for the group.

DISCUSSION Adding a coverage group to a class as part of an extension is called an introduction. Once the class extension has been made, no special syntax is required to actually make the introduction.

However, unlike the introduction of methods, fields, constraints, and events, the name of the coverage group must be unique across all extensions of the class (see "How do I extend a coverage group?" on page 46 for an explanation). Because the name of a cover group is the name of the event that triggers it, this means that you have to name your events carefully. The best option is just to add the determinant values into the event name.

EXAMPLE The following code is illegal because the new cover groups have the same name, even though they are in different subtypes.

```
extend CONTROL packet_s{
  event cover_e;
  routable: bool;

  cover cover_e{
    item routable;
  };
};

extend PAYLOAD packet_s{
  event cover_e;
  data: uint;

  cover cover_e{
    item data;
  };
};
```

The following code does work:

```
extend CONTROL packet_s{
  event cover_control_e;
  routable: bool;

  cover cover_control_e{
    item routable;
  };
};

extend PAYLOAD packet_s{
  event cover_payload_e;
  data: uint;

  cover cover_payload_e{
    item data;
  };
};
```

2.6 How do I extend a coverage group?

PROBLEM　　I want to extend a coverage group that is defined in a base class.

```
extend <DETERMINANTs> <CLASS NAME>{
  cover <GROUP> using also <OPTIONS> is also{
    <COVER EXTENSION>
  };
};
```

SOLUTION

■ <CLASS NAME> is the name of the class you want to extend.

■ <DETERMINANTs> are the determinant values under which you want the extension to occur.

■ <GROUP> is the name of the cover group you want to extend.

- <OPTIONS> are optional, and contain the new options for the cover group.

- <COVER EXTENSIONS> are optional and can define your new coverage items and/or change existing coverage items.

Note that using also and is also are both optional, so the following variations can be used:

```
// Add advice to the group but no introductions
//
extend <DETERMINANTs> <CLASS NAME>{
  cover <GROUP> using also <OPTIONS>;
};

// Either:
// a) Add introductions but no advice to the
// group
// b) Add advice to an existing item in the
// group
//
extend <DETERMINANTs> <CLASS NAME>{
  cover <GROUP> is also{
    <COVER EXTENSION>
  };
};
```

DISCUSSION   Coverage groups can only be extended with the using also and is also keywords. As discussed earlier, using also is for adding advice, and is also is for making introductions.

It is important to understand that Specman handles coverage group extension differently from other types of extension. When you introduce a new field, method, constraint, or event to a subtype, Specman keeps these apart from each other. They are only visible when the determinants have the correct value, and introductions in one subtype cannot interact with introductions in other subtypes.

This is not true for coverage groups. With these, Specman takes all of the cover groups in the class and when-subtypes and merges those with the same sampling event. Therefore, when you add new items to a cover group in a subtype, you have to ensure that the new item name is unique within the similarly sampled cover groups in the base class and all of the other subtypes. If an item appears more than once in a cover group when it is considered across the base class and all subtypes, then a compile-time error occurs.

Even if there are no other extensions to the cover group, it is best to take precautions now to prevent future problems. When you add a new item to a cover group, change its name to include the determinant values to ensure it is unique across all subtypes of the class. For instance, consider the following class with two subtypes. Each subtype extends the cover group to include a field that they have each introduced. This field has the same name in both subtypes. A compile-time error will occur because current_block appears in the finished_e cover block for both the LLP and RELOAD subtypes:

```
struct dma_transfer_s{
  event finished_e;
};

extend LLP dma_transfer_s{
  current_block : uint;
  cover finished_e{
    item current_block;
  };
};

extend RELOAD dma_transfer_s{
  current_block : uint;
  cover finished_e{
    item current_block;
  };
};
```

The reason for this error becomes obvious when you consider that Specman will merge the cover groups. This is what Specman sees internally:

```
cover finished_e{
   item current_block;
   item current_block;
};
```

To get this to work, you have to give the `current_block` items unique names as follows:

```
extend LLP dma_transfer_s{
  current_block : uint;
  cover finished_e{
    item llp_current_block: uint = current_block;
  };
};

extend RELOAD dma_transfer_s{
  current_block : uint;
  cover finished_e{
    item reload_current_block: uint = current_block;
  };
};
```

There will be no error here, because after the merge, Specman sees

```
cover finished_e{
   item llp_current_block;
   item reload_current_block;
};
```

2.7   How do I change the behavior of a method?

PROBLEM   I want to change the behavior of an existing method. How do I do this?

SOLUTION   You can add advice to the method before and/or after it executes, or you can replace the method completely.

```
extend <DETERMINANTs> <CLASS NAME>{
  // Add behavior to the start of a method
  //
  <METHOD PROTOTYPE> is first{
  };

  // Replace a method completely
  //
  <METHOD PROTOTYPE> is only{
  };

  // Add behavior to the end of a method
  //
  <METHOD PROTOTYPE> is also{
  };
};
```

- ■ <CLASS NAME> is the name of the class you want to extend.

- ■ <DETERMINANTs> are the determinant values under which you want the advice to occur.

- ■ <METHOD PROTOTYPE> is the prototype of the method you want to extend.

DISCUSSION   The functionality added to the start or the end of a method, or that replaces the original method completely, is called advice. If you want to alter the functionality of the method by preprocessing its parameters or postprocessing its results, then is first or is also can be used. If you need to change behavior that is embedded within the original method, then you'll have to replace the method entirely using is only. An is only advice will replace the original method *and* all of the other advice added up until this point.

You can add multiple advice to a method, but you cannot easily control the order in which these advice are executed. See "Controlling the order of method extension calls" on page 65 for more information about this.

Advice is simply a method that is hooked into the start or end of an existing method, possibly replacing the original method, so it can declare local variables, if required. However, these are not visible to other advice on the root method or the root method itself. Only the me and result variables are shared across advice. The method's parameters are shared across advice, and any changes made to a parameter's value are passed on as well.

Note: Be careful when using return in a method or in an advice. Its behavior may not be what you expect. See "Using return in method advice" on page 59 for more information.

EXAMPLE

```
struct packet_s{
  init() is {
    outf("Initializing packet_s\n");
  };
};
```

This executes to give

```
Initialising packet_s
```

Now we will add an is first and an is also advice.

```
extend packet_s{
   init() is first{
     outf("packet_s.init() is first\n");
   };
   init() is also{
     outf("packet_s.init() is also\n");
   };
};
```

This executes to give

```
packet_s.init() is first
Initializing packet_s
packet_s.init() is also
```

Now we will add another is first and another is also advice.

```
extend packet_s{
   init() is first{
     outf("packet_s.init() is first (2)\n");
   };
   init() is also{
     outf("packet_s.init() is also (2)\n");
   };
};
```

This executes to give

```
packet_s.init() is first (2)
packet_s.init() is first
Initializing packet_s
packet_s.init() is also
packet_s.init() is also (2)
```

If we add an `is only` advice, then the original functionality and all of the advice added so far will be replaced.

```
extend packet_s{
  init() is only{
    outf("packet_s.init() is only\n");
  };
};
```

This executes to give

```
packet_s.init() is only
```

2.8 How do I limit the scope of my extensions?

PROBLEM   I am about to extend a class that other verification components use as well, for example, the AHB verification component from Cadence, and I want to limit the scope of the
changes to just my verification component.

SOLUTION   Define a type called `<prefix>_project_name_t` with one
value called NONE, and add that to *all* shared classes you
intend to extend. This will be used as a determinant to limit
all future extensions to just instances of the class that have
your project name as the value. `<prefix>` will be your company prefix and a project-specific prefix. The project-specific
prefix is needed because you are extending the class globally,
so without this prefix, you might clash with other projects
that are using the same technique.

It is easy to add this field, but it can be tricky to propa-
gate its value down a class hierarchy. It's not impossible
though, and once it's done, everyone can enjoy the benefits. The following code shows how this can be done using

the slave agent and the slave signal map from Cadence's
AHB eVC:

```
extend vr_ahb_slave {
  soc2005_project_name : project_name_t;
  keep soft soc2005_project_name    == NONE;
  keep ssmp.soc2005_project_name    ==
                  value(soc2005_project_name);

  keep config.soc2005_project_name  ==
                     value(soc2005_project_name);

  keep monitor.soc2005_project_name ==
                     value(soc2005_project_name);
};

extend vr_ahb_slave_signal_map {
  soc2005_project_name : soc2005_project_name_t;
  keep soft soc2005_project_name == NONE;
};
```

In your project, create a unique value for this type and use it
when extending classes. For instance,

```
extend soc2005_project_name_t : [SoC2005];
extend SoC2005 S1 vr_ahb_slave_signal_map {
  // Some signal binds
};
```

This example extends the signal map type for the AHB slave
s1, but only in your project, SoC2005. Anyone else using a
slave s1 in another project will not see your extensions.

DISCUSSION   A class extension has a global scope. When you're working
in the splendid isolation of your module level verification
environment, writing your eVC and merrily making all the
extensions you need, this will probably not be an issue
for you. However, as soon as your eVC goes into a larger

verification environment you can expect problems. Here are some examples of problems you can have:

- Member name collision;

- Predefined determinant name collision;

- Feature leak;

- Functionality clash;

- Namespace pollution.

Member name collision

If you extend a class and add new members, then you have to be sure that their names are unique for the determinants you used in the extension (if you used any at all). If another extension with the same determinant values also uses these names, then you'll get a compiler error. For example, the following code will have problems:

```
// Code from project A
//
extend axi_master{
  unique_name: ver_unique_name_type;
};

// Code from project B
//
extend axi_master{
  unique_name: string;
};
```

The compiler will see that `axi_master` has two properties with the same name, and this isn't allowed.

The best way to solve this is to use a project-specific determinant field:

```
// Code from project A
//
extend PROJECT_A axi_master{
  unique_name: ver_unique_name_type;
};

// Code from project B
//
extend PROJECT_B axi_master{
  unique_name: string;
};
```

Predefined determinant name collision

Some eVCs come with a set of predefined determinant values. For example, the Cadence AHB eVC uses S0, S1, S2, etc., to identify slave instances. If you just use these predefined determinants to extend your classes, you are almost guaranteed a collision when you add your eVC to a system level verification environment. For example,

```
// Code from project A
//
extend S1 vr_ahb_slave_signal_map {
  // Some signal binds
};

// Code from project B
//
extend S1 vr_ahb_slave_signal_map {
  // Some other signal binds.
  // PROBLEM: These signal binds will clash
  // with the signal binds from project A
};
```

Feature leak

Feature leak happens when behavior that should have been added for just one instance of a class is actually added to all instances of the class. The results of this might be annoying and slow down the simulation, but they will not impact the verification quality.

Perhaps you have set up your slave monitor to print a formatted message whenever one of its transfers completes on the bus.

```
extend slave_monitor {
  on transfer_ended{
    outf("Transfer finished:\n");
    outf("   -> address   = %x\n",
                               transfer.address);
    outf("   -> register = %s\n",
          get_register_name(transfer.address));
    outf("   -> data      = %x\n",
                               transfer.data);
    outf("   -> response = %s\n",
              transfer.response.as_a(string));
  };
};
```

That was probably fine when you only had one slave agent in your verification environment. The problem now is that at the system level, you have 30 or 40 slave agents in your verification environment, and they're all now printing this message. Not only that, but the call to `get_register_name()` will be returning some pretty useless results for the slave interfaces shadowing other modules. Although this isn't a fatal problem, it's something you could live without.

Functionality clash

This is a variation of feature leak but one that can affect the verification quality. Here, functionality from one class instance clashes with the functionality from other instances and adversely affects their operation. For example, a class extension prevents other instances of the class from performing the checks that they need to do or from injecting the stimuli that they need to inject.

As an example, sometimes people extend classes to switch off features they don't want. For example, assume your AHB module doesn't return SPLIT responses, so you extend the slave sequence so that it can't return SPLITS. If you extend the slave sequence globally then you have just switched off SPLIT responses from all slaves in the system — even those on other buses when SPLITS are needed to test the arbiter.

A common cause of functionality clash is that people extend third-party eVCs to configure them. Take the example of a UART eVC, which stores the configuration as follows:

```
type parity_type_t is : [NONE, EVEN, ODD];
struct uart_config_s{
  parity : parity_type_t;
  keep soft parity == NONE;
};
```

Now in your design, you only have one UART and it has no parity, so you just accept the default constraint.

However, when you build a system level verification environment that contains your design and its UART, along with another design and its UART, a problem appears. Your UART suddenly starts transmitting with even parity. Why?

Because the eVC for the other design configures its UART eVC with the following code:

```
extend uart_config_s{
  keep parity == EVEN;
};
```

Namespace pollution

This is an aesthetic problem, but it can cause confusion during debug. You have extended a common class and during a simulation you use the data browser, or maybe just print, to view the class. The problem is that the class will now contain the fields and methods introduced by other eVCs, so you are faced with a confusing welter of information that you have to try and ignore.

2.9 Using `return` in method advice

PROBLEM I'm returning from an advice and the behavior I see is not what I expected. What's going on?

SOLUTION Never use `return` in an `is first` advice, and remember that a `return` from the root method or an advice only stops the execution of the root method or that advice. The remaining advice are still called …

… unless the advice that had a `return` was an `is first`, in which case only some of the remaining advice are called.

DISCUSSION Putting the `return` keyword into a method traditionally means that you want to return from that method. In almost all programming languages it is that simple. Advice makes it more complex in *e*, and the ability for other people to later extend your code means that it may be worth avoiding the `return` keyword altogether.

The numbers indicate the
order the advice were
declared in the code

| is first (5) |

| is first (3) |

| method |

| is also (1) |

| is also (2) |

| is also (4) |

Order of execution

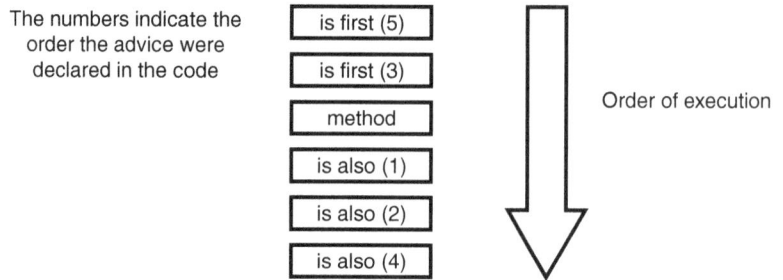

Figure 2.2   What really happens when a method
is called.

When you call a method in *e*, you are actually calling a list[14]
containing the root method and the advice (Figure 2.2).
The `is` `first` advice will be at the start of the list, the `is`
`also` advice at the end, and the root method will be somewhere in the between the two. When the *e* compiler encoun-
ters an `is first` advice it adds it to the start of the list, which
is why the later they are declared, the earlier they get called.
The `is` `also` advice are added to the end of the list, which is
why they are called in the order they appear in the code.

A root method or an advice with a `return` in it will always
return, but the list will continue to get processed. However,
the next item in the list to get processed depends on how the
return happened and what type of advice returned. Figure
2.3 shows a flow chart that shows how the *e* compiler builds
up the execution list for a method.

---

[14] Actually, it's more complex than this. Because some advice might be
present in classes only under certain conditions (set by the determinants), a
graph is needed to work out the order in which the root method and its extensions get called. The graph looks like a finite state machine, where each state is
the root method or its advice, and the transition from one state to another can
only happen if the determinants have the correct values.

However, this added complexity adds nothing but pain to the discussion, so I
will (thankfully) ignore it.

```
                    ┌──────────────────┐
                    │  Process method  │
                    │    or advice     │
                    └────────┬─────────┘
                             │
         is also           ◇ kind          is first
                    ┌──────────────┐
```

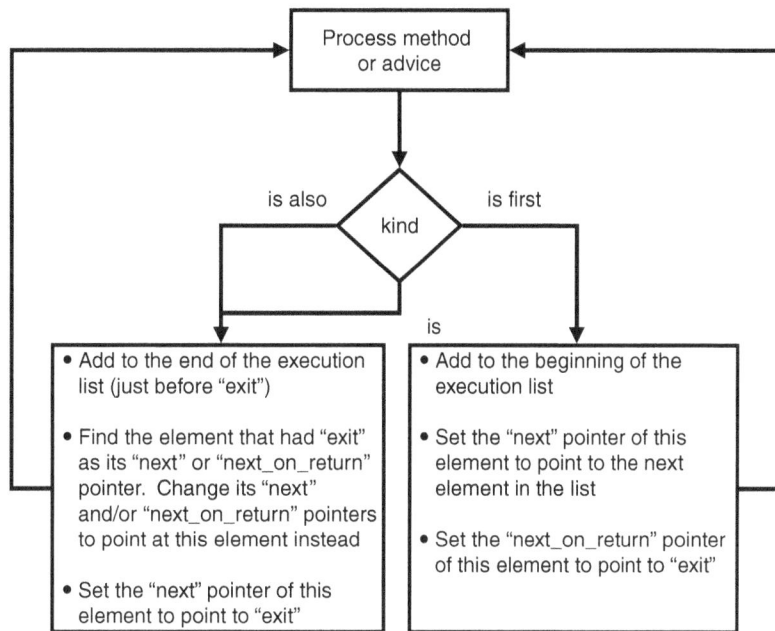

Figure 2.3   What will get called when you mix return with advice?

To understand the flowchart, imagine that the execution list is a linked list, where each element has one or two next item pointers. One points to the list element to be executed next if the root method or advice exits naturally (the `next` pointer). The other points to the list element to be executed next if the root method or advice returns because of a `return` statement (the `next_on_return` pointer). Two pointers are needed in case the `return` statement is selected conditionally at runtime. Only `is first` advice has the `next_on_return` pointer.

The "exit" element is the last entry in the list. It is merely a placeholder that allows us to set the `next` and `next_on_return` pointers to something when a list element is the last to be executed. It's a bit like the "\0" string terminator in C.

The following example shows the flowchart in action.

EXAMPLE   The code shows a sequence of advice added to a root method called `foo`. The root method, and each of the advice, prints a message with a number in it. The number simply designates the order in which the method or advice appeared in the code. The comments in the code refer to Figure 2.4. This figure shows how the execution list builds up as new advice is parsed from the code.

```
<'
extend sys{
  // The root method. See point (a)
  //
  foo() is{
    outf("foo() is(0)\n");
  };

  // See point (b)
  //
  foo() is also{
    outf("foo() is also(1)\n");
  };

  // See point (c)
  //
  foo() is first{
    outf("foo() is first(2)\n");
  };

  // This advice has a return statement. The
  // next_on_return pointer will always be
  // used. See point (d)
  //
  foo() is first{
    outf("foo() is first(3)\n");
    return;
  };

  // This advice has a return statement. The
  // next pointer will be used, because is also
```

```
// advice does not have a next_on_return
// pointer. See point (e)
//
foo() is also{
  outf("foo() is also(4)\n");
  return;
};

// This advice has a conditional return
// statement. Both the next and the next_on_
// return pointers will be used. See point
// (f)
//
flag: bool;
foo() is first{
  outf("foo() is first(5)\n");
  outf("flag = %s\n", flag);

  if(flag == TRUE){
   outf("Returning from foo is first(5)\n");
   return;
  };
};

// This extension shows that no matter what
// has happened earlier, subsequent
// extensions will still be called.
// See point (g)
//
foo() is also{
  outf("foo() is also(6)\n");
};

// Method foo is called
//
run() is also{
  foo();
  };
};
'>
```

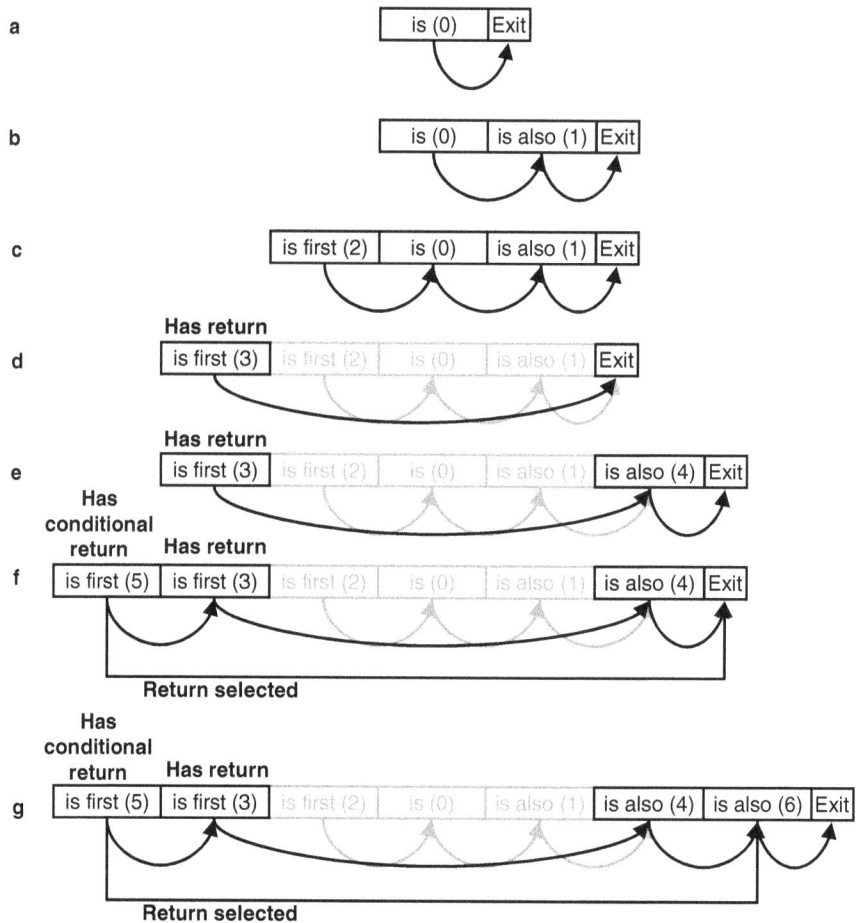

Figure 2.4   How the execution list changes as
more code is parsed.

The first interesting thing to note in the execution list is
the difference between points c and d. Both of these had
is first advice added. The is first advice added at point c
doesn't have a return statement in it, so the advice just gets
added to the start of the list. However, the is first advice at
point d does have a return statement, so the entire execution
list is replaced with just this advice.

The second interesting thing occurs at point f, because
the is first advice added here has a conditional return.

The return statement is only selected when `flag == TRUE`. Because the advice has a path through it with no return keyword, the list is not reset. However, if the return is taken, then the list acts as if it has been reset. The following shows the output for both paths:

When `flag == FALSE`:

```
foo() is first(5)
flag = TRUE
Returning from is first(5)
foo() is also(6)
```

When `flag == TRUE`:

```
foo() is first(5)
flag = FALSE
foo() is first(3)
foo() is also(4)
foo() is also(6)
```

2.10   Controlling the order of method extension calls

There are two options open to you to control the order that your extensions are called in:

- You can control the call order by controlling the order the extensions are loaded;

- You can use hook methods to build a sequencer.

It's very hard to define the order in which all of the extensions to a particular root method are called. One option is to carefully specify the order the files are loaded in. `is also` extensions are executed in the order that they are loaded, and `is first` are executed in the reverse order in which they were loaded (see "Using `return` in method advice" on page 59). This approach can become complex, may require highly fragmented files, and is very fragile. Anyone refactoring the manifest[15] file will break the code, possibly with very subtle results.

If it's important that all of your `is first` (or `is also`) extensions to a particular method are called in a fixed order, use a sequencer, which you'll find defined in Chapter 4.

---

[15] A *manifest file* is simply a file containing a list of other files. It is commonly known as a "top" file in *e*.

3

Using AOP to Organize Your Code

What was new, though, was the realization that "patching done right" is the most natural way to understand complex systems.

Ivar Jacobson [22]

Unless you plan to have your entire verification environment coded in a single file (and please don't) then you'll have to decide, fairly early on in the design process, how you are going to map your code to files. If you are used to object oriented programming, then you are probably used to mapping entire classes to files. Class Foo probably got placed in foo.cpp (assuming C++ code), and class Bar probably got placed in bar.cpp. You might have used header files as well as a body file, and if you did, you might have used several body files for a particularly large class. So, for instance, the header for Foo would be in foo.hpp and the body in foo_1.cpp and foo_2.cpp. You might have had a slightly different variation, but conventional wisdom for OOP programmers is to have one class per file and have the file name be the name of the class.

As far as it goes, it's a good approach. However, it does presume that you consider the class to be the most important way of organizing and viewing your code. That is, it assumes that you care more about isolating all of the code for class Foo than you do about, say, isolating all of the code that deals with monitoring or checking. That always strikes me as a bit odd. After all, monitoring and checking are my goals; classes are just something I need to make them happen. The truth is that I don't *really* care about having all of class Foo in a single file or being able to find all of it quickly. Class Foo will contain parts of many crosscutting concerns and there's seldom a reason to look at all of these together.

AOP, on the other hand, lets you organize your code by aspect, and aspects can be *anything you like*. That means that you're no longer limited to organizing your code by class — you can do it by functionality, which is something that I consider much more important. Of course, you can still organize it by class if you want,[16] or by class *and* by functionality, or by any other scheme or combination of schemes that interests you (see "What aspects do I want to use?" on page 70 for more information). The following are some advantages you can get by changing the way you organize your code:

- It can be easier to find particular pieces of code. You don't know what class connects the scoreboards to the monitors? Who cares? — look for code in the scoreboard and monitor aspects.

- It can be easier to isolate code for review. You want to review all BFMs? Isolate the files in the BFM aspect and tell someone to look at them.

- It can be easier to assign to people to work on particular functionality. Not only can you assign people to particular aspects (as mentioned earlier), but you can have multiple people working on the same aspect

---

[16] You might have spotted that the OOP approach discussed above is just the case where you only care about one aspect, and that's the classes in your testbench.

without getting involved in revision control merges (which can, frankly, be a complete pain at times).

■ You can encapsulate your crosscutting concerns and remove the code scattering and tangling problems.

■ It's easier to reuse code, because you can separate the core functionality (which is where you add value) from the infrastructure needed to tie it to a particular verification environment.

One of the first questions you'll need to answer when you begin coding your verification environment is, "What aspects do I want to use?"

3.1   A word about style

But before I answer that though, let me digress a bit, because structuring your code any way you like it can be a double-edged sword if you aren't careful. The most common reason I've heard for not using AOP is that it creates incomprehensible spaghetti code. I don't agree with this, and I'll explain why in Chapter 7. The simple truth is that bad programmers create bad code, and they'll do it no matter what language or methodology they use.

It is fair to say, however, that AOP lacks an *obvious* way of doing it right. I haven't seen a methodology anywhere for structuring your AOP code. Because of this it is unfortunately common to see people making extensions in any file that happens to be open in their editor, and as long as the compilation dependencies are satisfied, they don't care. File by file, line by line, the code base of the verification environment is transformed into a tangled mess that is virtually impossible to unpick. But it doesn't have to be this way. By storing code properly when it is created, it becomes quite simple to find it later. I only have two requirements for organizing AOP code:

Requirement 1:   You should be able to easily find all code relating to an aspect.

Requirement 2:   You should be able to add or remove an aspect from the verification environment without modifying any existing code.

The following rules will help you meet these requirements:

- The name of a file should describe the contents of the file;

- The contents of a file should match its name;

- Wherever possible, minimize the number of concerns in a single file. The more concerns that appear in one file, the more tightly coupled they become, and this makes it harder to remove and replace them.

By following these rules, religiously and in a worryingly obsessive manner, it will be easy to find all of the pieces of code that apply to your aspects. It will also be easy to remove and replace aspects (Chapter 5, "Creating Pluggable Code").

3.2   What aspects do I want to use?

Remember from a previous discussion that aspects are simply views of your code base, and to get hold of a particular view, you have to "ask" for it. I likened this to executing a database search, with the result being your aspect. To be able to do this, you have to store your code in such a way that the code matching the search query can be identified. This book covers two different ways of doing this (see this chapter and "8.12. Finding aspects" on page 231), but for now, let's ignore the technical details of *how* you match code to the search query, and let's look at how you might go about deciding *what* you want to be able to search for. Let's look at how you might decide what your aspects should be. Making your code searchable to create different views requires manual steps,[17] and this will limit the number of aspects you will have. How do you chose these?

Identifying aspects can be difficult, and there are no hard and fast rules. It is similar to the old OOP quandary — how do I design a class? After 20 plus years, there is still no definitive set of rules to follow. The truth is that some people can just "see" classes and aspects when reading a specification — they simply leap out at them — but others have to work to identify them. There are some guidelines that might help though. When you are planning your verification environment, or refactoring some code, ask yourself the following questions:

Is this something I want to find again easily?

Some code could live happily in a number of different locations in your verification environment. For example, the code that adds a transaction to a scoreboard could be put into the monitor that generates the transaction, and the monitor pushes the transaction into the scoreboard when it is ready. Alternatively, the code that adds the transaction could be in the scoreboard, and the scoreboard pulls it from the monitor when it is ready. Presented with a file called scoreboard.sv

---

[17] Imagine that you did have some form of database that held your code. To be able to search the code using database queries, you would have had to manually assign the code to different search values anyway. For example, when you added some lines of code that implemented functional coverage for an OCP slave, you would somehow have to have said, "this code should match searches for OCP, Slave, and Functional Coverage." My point here is that even with such a tool, the manual steps required would still limit the number of aspects you could have, so you would still need to carefully decide what they should be before entering your code into the tool.

and a file called `monitor.cpp`, where should you look for this code?

AOP lets you handle this differently. If you really did care about this, you could create an aspect that dealt with communication between the monitor and the scoreboard and have the code in that aspect. If you did that, you could always find the code instantly, without even caring which class, monitor, or scoreboard, it was in.

If you think that this example is a bit unrealistic, then let's look at another (although I have actually used that aspect — you'll see why in Chapter 5, "Creating Pluggable Code"). Functional coverage has many potential homes. You might find some in your tests, sequence items, or transactions, some in your BFMs, some in your monitors, and some in your checkers. It tends to appear wherever you have something that you might want to cover. Now say you want to find all of your functional coverage at some stage; perhaps you want to improve the item names so that your reports make more sense. Having functional coverage as an aspect means you can do this instantly without having to hunt through all of the classes in your design, just in case some ended up in there.

Is this something I want to conditionally include at compile time?

Sometimes you only want to include code in the verification environment under certain compile-time conditions. For instance, if you are compiling the verification environment to interact with an RTL design, you do not want to include any code that interfaces to a SystemC model of the design.

The traditional approach to this would be to surround the appropriate sections of code with `#ifdef` statements. However, this can obfuscate the source code, making it harder to read. Using AOP, we can encapsulate the different code in separate files (which is one way of creating physical aspects), and just put the `#ifdef` statements into the manifest file. This makes the source code cleaner and makes it more obvious what code will be included in a simulation. You can see what will be included just by looking at the manifest file. The following code fragment shows a possible manifest file for the example in Figure 7.7 (on page 186).

```
<'
import bfm;
#ifdef USE_RTL{
   import bfm-connect_layer-rtl;
};
#ifdef USE_ACCELERATOR{
   import bfm-connect_layer-accelerator;
};
'>
```

Is this something I want to isolate so I can assign it to someone?

Sometimes you just need to isolate some code and ask someone else to work on it. The code may be part of a crosscutting concern ("add loggers to all units," "add system wide support for the control packet") or might just be part of a single class ("Can you add address translation to this BFM while I'm working on the burst calculations?").

The advantage AOP brings here is that you can split the work required on a class and pass it to different people who can work on it in parallel without affecting each other or having to mess around with your configuration management software.

Is this something I want to isolate for review purposes?

Perhaps you want to hold a special review for the code you are looking at. It might be the code that deals with end-of-test handling, and you want to review that separately to make sure the tests end correctly. Perhaps you want to check that no extensions to third-party verification components will cause namespace collisions with other code that extends these components. Put the code in an aspect and have the appropriate team members review just that aspect. This allows you to split the code review into distinct areas of functionality and invite just the appropriate experts.

Is this dangerous code I can't afford to forget about?

Sometimes you have to put code into a verification environment to turn off error messages or avoid certain areas of functionality while you're waiting for a bug to be fixed (see "6.3. Handling workarounds" on page 149). This code is dangerous. If you forget about it and leave it in the verification environment, then there's a very good chance of releasing an unverified design.

To avoid this risk, put the code into an aspect and store it somewhere obvious. For example,

```
my_evc/e/review_before_release/workarounds.e
```

Is this something that is obviously sliceable?

Does this code just look like a sliceable piece of functionality? Perhaps it is a new variation of an existing packet type, a new CPU OP code, or a new ALU instruction. It is almost certain that supporting this will require changes to the BFM, sequences, scoreboards, and coverage. Group all of these changes together in an aspect. Chapter 5, "Creating Pluggable Code" talks about this in much more detail.

Does this code prevent me from reusing the class/agent/eVC?

Are you looking at something that isn't portable to a new verification environment? It could be an access to a central resource database, an environment variable, a definition of the design's topology, or simply a hard coded path from sys to your agent. If you can't guarantee that the code will remain valid in all potential verification environments, then leaving it in your verification component will lock the component to one verification environment. Instead, separate it as an aspect that has to be rewritten when the code is ported to a new verification environment.

Do I want/need to make this change noninvasively?

If the code you are about to write affects some other code, and you can't or don't want to modify that code directly, use AOP to patch it. Once you are happy with the patch, roll it in with the existing code base.

3.3   Mapping aspects to files

If you followed the guidelines in "What aspects do I want to use?" on page 70, you'll know what aspects you want to work with in your verification environment. Remember from "What are aspects — Part II" on page 27 that an aspect is a particular view of your code. I said that if you thought about your code in terms of a database, a database query would be the conceptual aspect and the code returned the physical aspect. So for instance, you could ask to see all the code dealing with functional coverage, or all the code where the AHB monitor and AHB scoreboard interact. These would be the functional coverage aspect and the AHB monitor-and-scoreboard aspect, respectively.

There are many conceptual aspects in your verification environment, but unless you make them explicit, you'll never be able to access them as physical aspects. Your task now is to make your chosen aspects explicit. This section describes a way of doing this that does not require support from external tools. However, it's only really useful if you do it before coding your verification environment or if you do a major refactoring of your existing verification environment, because it uses files to make your chosen conceptual aspects physical. If this isn't possible (or if you decide you don't want to do it this way), then an alternative way is described in "8.12. Finding aspects" on page 231.

To access the database you need a key, and the key is simply the list of aspects you want to see (functional coverage, AHB monitor, AHB scoreboard, etc.). We need to define up-front the aspects we are interested in and manually organize the code to match. The way to do this is to build the key into the file name and make sure the contents of the file are only associated with the aspects named in the file name. The file name should be split into sections, where each section contains the name of an aspect that the file contributes to. The format is as follows:

```
<aspect 1>-<aspect 2>-<aspect 3> ... <aspect n>.e
```

The "..." just shows that there may be more aspect names and should not itself appear in the file name. Aspect names can also contain the "_" character, such as `functional_coverage`.

As an example, imagine you had the following aspects (Figure 3.1)

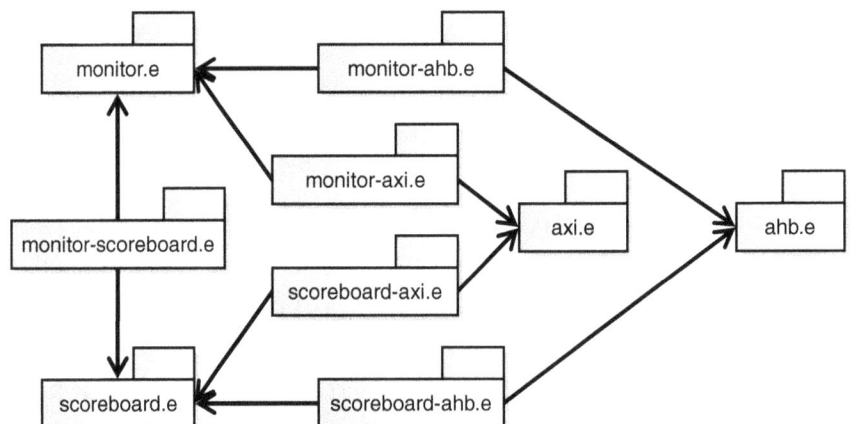

Figure 3.1   AOP file structure for the example.

- Monitor: All code dealing with monitoring;

- Scoreboard: All code dealing with scoreboards;

- AHB: All code dealing with the AHB bus protocol;

- AXI: All code dealing with the AXI bus protocol;

and the following files:[18]

- monitor.e: Contains the generic monitor class, defining the links to the agent, the reset behavior and the communication mechanism;

- scoreboard.e: Contains the generic scoreboard class, defining the links to the agent, the reset behavior, the communication mechanism, the history logs, and the methods called to add and compare transactions;

- ahb.e: Contains type definitions for the AHB protocol;

- axi.e: Contains type definitions for the AHB protocol;

- monitor-ahb.e: Contains the monitor specializations needed to monitor the AHB protocol;

- scoreboard-ahb.e: Contains the scoreboard specializations needed to check the AHB protocol;

- monitor-axi.e: Contains the monitor specializations needed to monitor the AXI protocol;

- scoreboard-axi.e: Contains the scoreboard specializations needed to check the AXI protocol;

- monitor-scoreboard.e: Contains the link between the generic monitor and the generic scoreboard.

---

[18] In a real project you might want to make these file names *e*RM compliant by adding a company prefix and a project prefix.

You can now take slices of the database using the Unix `ls` and `grep` commands:

To isolate all monitor code (Figure 3.2):

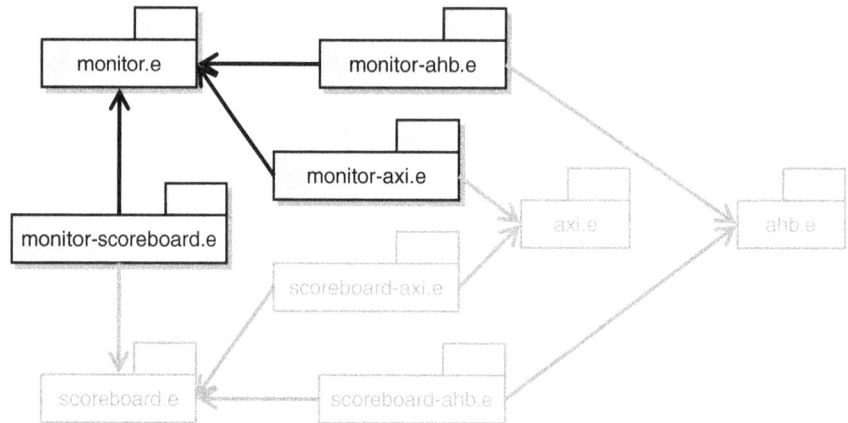

Figure 3.2   AOP file structure showing the monitor aspect.

```
ls | grep monitor
monitor.e
monitor-ahb.e
monitor-axi.e
monitor-scoreboard.e
```

To isolate all AHB code (Figure 3.3):

```
ls | grep ahb
ahb.e
monitor-ahb.e
scoreboard-ahb.e
```

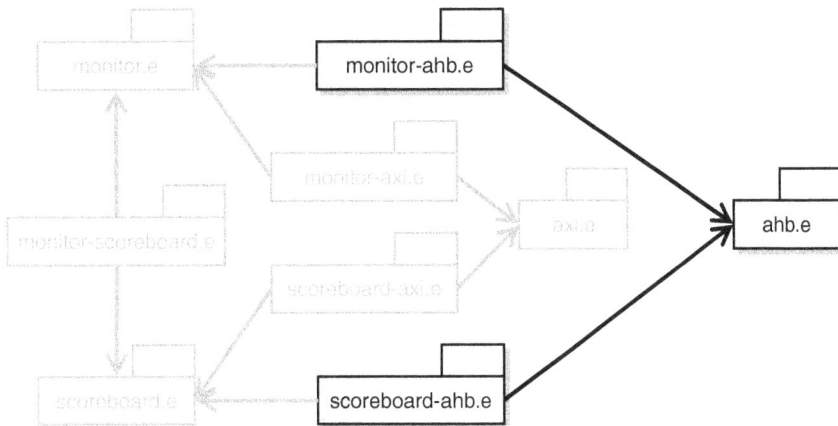

Figure 3.3   AOP file structure showing the AHB
aspect.

To see all code where the monitors and scoreboards interact
(Figure 3.4):

```
ls | grep monitor | grep scoreboard
```

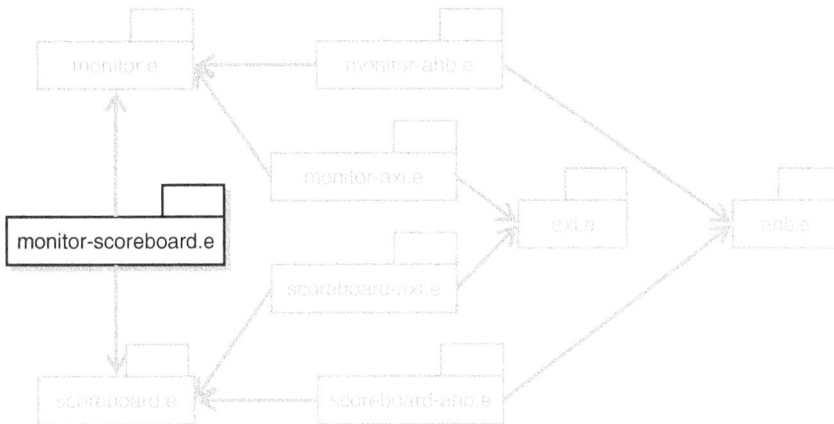

Figure 3.4   AOP file structure showing the
combined monitor and scoreboard aspect.

At this stage, I've shown you a method of naming your files
so that you can easily find code, but I haven't told you yet
how to come up with the files in the first place.

Let's look at how we could structure the files for the following selection:

- Monitor: All code dealing with monitoring;
- Scoreboard: All code dealing with scoreboards;
- AHB: All code dealing with the AHB protocol;
- AXI: All code dealing with the AXI protocol.

If you decided that you didn't want to have lots of files, you could try to structure the code as shown in Figure 3.5. Within each of these aspect files you can define multiple classes, extensions, advice, and introductions to help keep the classes separate from each other. In this example the AXI scoreboard is instantiated in the original AXI monitor, so no extension is required.

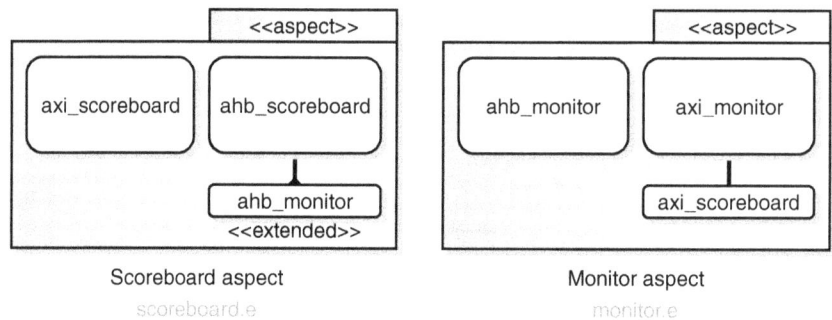

Figure 3.5   Trying to minimize files.

```
// Declare the axi_monitor. This instantiates the
// axi_scoreboard
//
struct axi_monitor{
  !scoreboard: axi_scoreboard;
```

```
  on transfer_finished{
    scoreboard.add_transfer(current_transfer);
  };
  // Other monitoring code goes here
};
```

Code Listing 2. Scoreboard code in the monitor aspect.

The situation is different for the AHB scoreboard. This requires extensions to the AHB monitor to connect the scoreboard and pass it finished transactions.

```
// Extend the monitor to add the link to the
// scoreboard
//
extend ahb_monitor{
  !scoreboard: ahb_scoreboard;

  on transfer_finished{
    scoreboard.add_transfer(current_transfer);
  };
};
```

Code Listing 3. Monitor code in the scoreboard aspect.

The scoreboard and monitor aspects look fairly well encapsulated, but the AHB and AXI are not encapsulated at all, because code for both of these appears in the same files. However, if you decide that finding monitor and scoreboard code is more important than finding AHB or AXI code, it's a good start.

It's a good start, but it's not actually a very good solution though, even for the scoreboard and monitor aspects. Take the `axi_monitor` and the `axi_scoreboard`. At some point these must interact with each other. Is it in the scoreboard.e file or the monitor.e file? Is it in both? The answer is that you just don't know without examining all of the files. Using just two files hasn't helped you encapsulate the code. You are still suffering from the code scattering problem. Both scoreboard.e and monitor.e have monitor and scoreboard code, although the *majority* of the code is in the right place.

Now say you wanted to remove the scoreboard aspect from the verification environment. Perhaps you want to run a batch of simulations to check your functional coverage and you aren't that bothered about checking the results. With this file structure, you can't remove the scoreboards without modifying monitor.e because it has some AXI scoreboard code.

Before I move onto solving the problems I've just discussed, let's look at a bigger problem, the AHB and AXI aspects, because there has been no attempt to encapsulate them at all. It is more likely that you will want to separate these aspects for reuse than you would the scoreboard and monitor aspects. Surely we can improve this situation? Of course we can, and the answer is to use more files. Figure 3.6 shows the new file

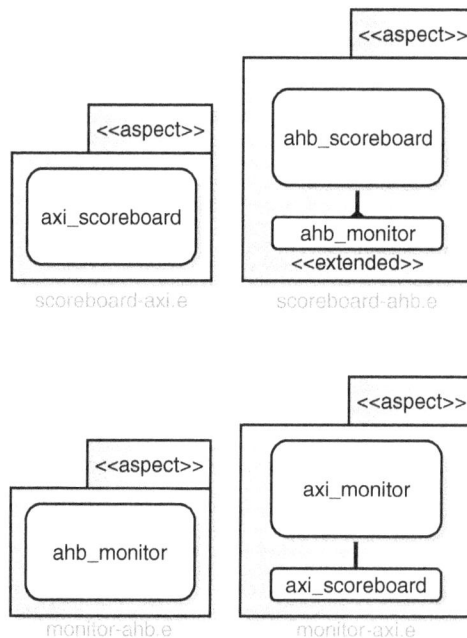

Figure 3.6   Separating the AHB and AXI aspects.

structure. Notice how the naming convention described earlier in this section has been used. This structure simply splits the AHB and AXI concerns into separate files.

Note there are no obvious aspect files anymore. In Figure 3.5 scoreboard.e was obviously the scoreboard aspect, and monitor.e was obviously the monitor aspect. The situation is less obvious when you move to more files. We can get the same effect though by choosing the file names wisely. By coding the aspect names into the file names, we can treat a selection of files as a single aspect, as shown in Figures 3.7 and 3.8. The multiple files that make up an aspect can be collated just using `ls` and `grep` as described earlier.

There are actually three aspects in Figure 3.7: the monitor-AHB aspect, the scoreboard-AHB aspect, and the AHB aspect, which contains the other two. Remember that an

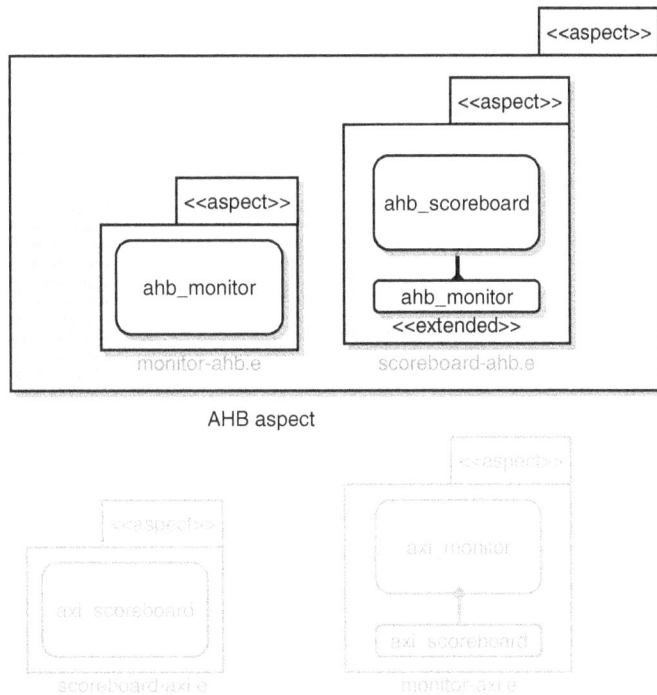

Figure 3.7 The AHB aspect.

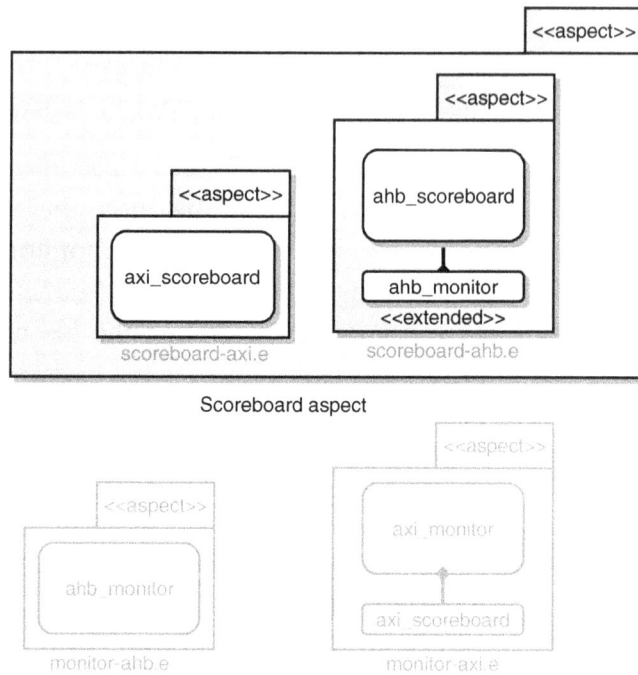

Figure 3.8   The scoreboard aspect.

aspect is just a particular view of your code. In this case, you want to view the AHB code, which includes the monitor-AHB aspect and the scoreboard-AHB aspect.

It's definitely a step in the right direction. By using multiple files to represent an aspect, I have managed to completely separate the AHB and AXI concerns. I can do this because they are completely orthogonal to each other. The same isn't true of the monitor and scoreboard aspects. These are crosscutting concerns. It is possible to make improvements here as well, though.

Back in the introduction to this section I mentioned that you should try to minimize the number of concerns that appear within a single file. In the example, the scoreboards are linked to the monitors. Rather than put the connection code in the scoreboard file or the monitor file, I will put it in a special file that is just used to connect these two aspects together. That way, if we change one of the aspects, only this special file has to be modified. I call this special file a *connector file*, because its only task is to connect aspects together. It shouldn't add any functionality — just infrastructure.

Figure 3.9 shows the final file structure for the example. The connector files are in the middle row. In Figure 3.9, I've used the size of the boxes used to represent the amount of functionality in a class. The bigger the box, the more functionality there is. This shows us that most of the functionality for an aspect lives outside of the connector files. Conversely, it shows that connector files should contain the minimum amount of functionality. This is important, because it is the connector files that will have to be rewritten if you change any of the aspects that they connect.

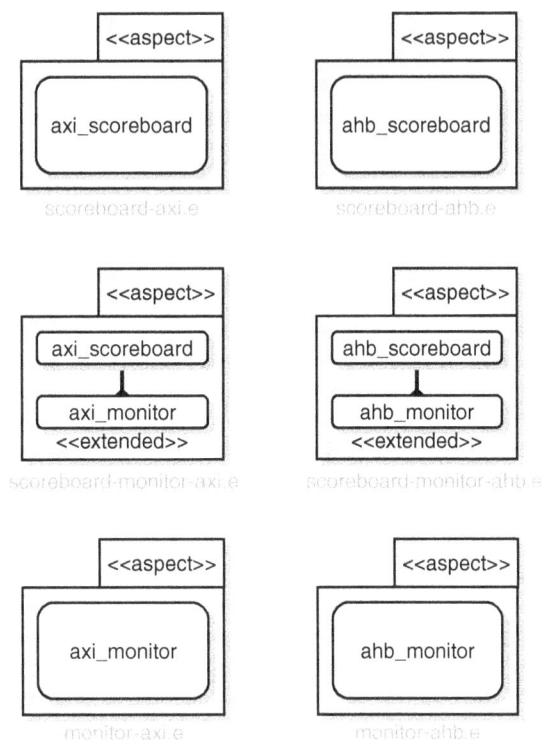

Figure 3.9 The final file set.

```
// Extend the monitor to add the link to the
// scoreboard
//
extend ahb_monitor{
  !scoreboard: ahb_scoreboard;

  on transfer_finished{
    scoreboard.add_transfer(current_transfer);
  };
};
```

Code Listing 4. The monitor-scoreboard-ahb connector file.

Figure 3.10 shows the files that make up the different aspects in the example. You may be asking yourself why I am defining the file where the AXI scoreboard meets the AXI monitor as a connector, but not the file where the AXI protocol meets the scoreboard aspect. The reason is that the AXI scoreboard has been coded as a dominant concern, so the AXI protocol and the scoreboard aspect are combined into one class. They are closely coupled, and there is no way to physically separate these two aspects with the architecture I have chosen, so having a connector between them doesn't make sense. It is different for the AXI scoreboard and the AXI monitor. These are both dominant concerns in their own rights — they have been coded as separate classes and are loosely coupled, so the connector file will contain references to both classes. The connector file just gives us a way of being able to localize the interaction between these dominant concerns, and lets us pull them apart later if required.

I find the following algorithm helpful when I'm trying to decide which file some code should go into:

1. Look at the line or block of code that you are dealing with and work out which aspect(s) it belongs to. Put the aspect names into a list in your head or on a scrap of

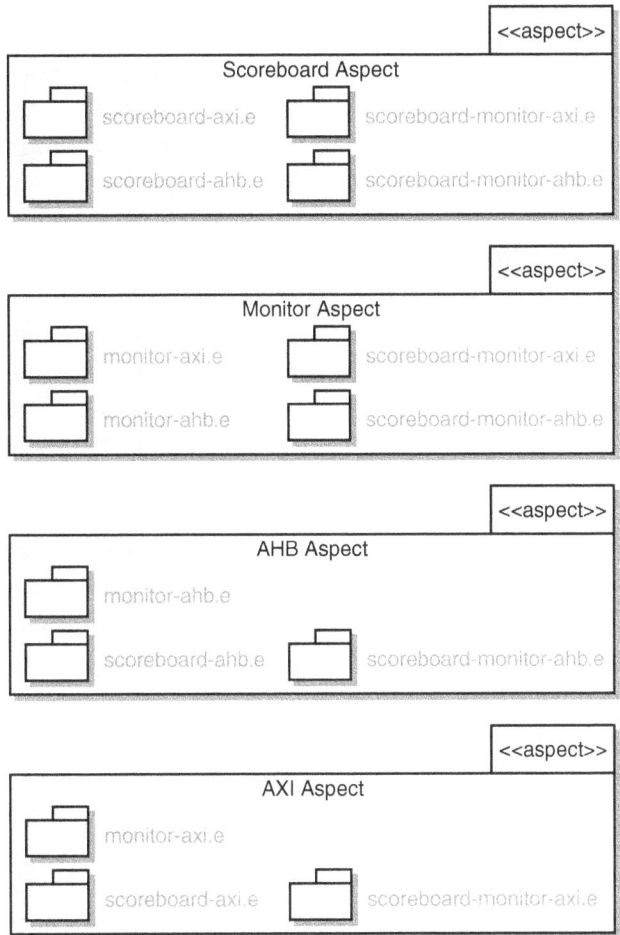

Figure 3.10   The various aspects.

paper. Keep processing contiguous lines that all belong to the same aspects. If you get to a line that doesn't map to *exactly* the same aspects in the list, go to step 2.

2. Remove any conceptual aspects from the list, because you are not using files to represent them.

3. If after removing the conceptual aspects the list is empty, then just put the code in the "class" file for the class that it belongs to. For example, if you find some functional coverage code being added to the monitor class, and you haven't identified functional coverage as a physical aspect,

then just put the code in monitor.e. If you encounter compilation problems due to dependencies when you do this, just create an additional body file for the class and put the code there. For example, you could create monitor 2.e, which gets loaded after the dependencies that caused the compilation problems.

4. After removing the conceptual aspects from the list, the list contains the names of the physical aspects that this code belongs to. Sort the list alphabetically. The code has to go into a file that contains all of these in the file name. For example, if the list was [AHB] [monitor] [scoreboard], then the code would go into ahb-monitor-scoreboard.e. When you move the code, you might have to do some refactoring to make sure that it still compiles. For example, code has to exist in a class block, and procedural code has to exist in a method.

5. Once you've moved the code, recompile and make sure everything still works. Then go back to step 1.

I'll apply the preceding algorithm to the following code fragment to give you a feel for how to do it. This code comes from the example we used earlier in this section, and the physical aspects I want to map it to are AHB, monitor, and scoreboard.

```
1. struct ahb_scoreboard{
2.   !source: ahb_master;
3.   !dest  : ahb_slave;
4.
5.   compare() is also{
6.     // Some AHB specific compare code in here.
7.   };
8. };
9.
10. extend ahb_monitor{
```

```
11.    cover transfer_finished is{
12.      item hburst: current_transfer.hburst;
13.      item hsize : current_transfer.hsize;
14.      // More AHB coverage
15.    };
16.    !scoreboard: ahb_scoreboard;
17.
18.    on transfer_finished{
19.      scoreboard.add_transfer(current_transfer);
20.    };
21. };
```

Code Listing 5. The unmapped code.

Starting at line 1 and step 1 of the algorithm, scan down the code, assigning it to aspects. Well, lines 1 to 8 all deal with AHB and scoreboarding, so the aspect list would be [AHB] and [Scoreboard]. Line 9 is empty and 10 deals with monitors, so we'll stop at line 8 and move on to step 2. Our list doesn't contain any conceptual aspects, so we can skip step 3 as well and move on to step 4. The list is already sorted alphabetically, so we can move the code into a file called ahb-scoreboard.e and return to step 1.

```
1. struct ahb_scoreboard{
2.    !source: ahb_master;
3.    !dest  : ahb_slave;
4.
5.    compare() is also{
6.      // Some AHB specific compare code in here.
7.    };
8. };
```

Code Listing 6. ahb-scoreboard.e.

Starting again at line 9 and step 1 of the algorithm, we are dealing with the monitor aspect. From lines 11 to 15 we are also dealing with functional coverage code, so our aspect list

so far is [AHB], [Monitor], and [Functional Coverage]. Line
16 deals with scoreboards, which isn't in our list, so we need
to move on to step 2. Note that we couldn't move to step 2 at
line 11 because this line will *always* be part of the monitor
aspect. Step 2 says we should discard the conceptual aspects,
which in this case is functional coverage. Although it's cer-
tainly a possible candidate for an aspect, in this example we
have chosen not to bother with it. This reduces the aspect list
to [AHB] and [Monitor]. That means that lines 10 to 15 get
put into ahb-monitor.e. This will require some refactoring
to ensure that the code continues to compile. The new lines
are shown in Code Listing 8 without any line numbers.

```
9.
10. extend ahb_monitor{
11.    cover transfer_finished is{
12.       item hburst: current_transfer.hburst;
13.       item hsize : current_transfer.hsize;
14.       // More AHB coverage
15.    };
16.    !scoreboard: ahb_scoreboard;
17.
18.    on transfer_finished{
19.      scoreboard.add_transfer(current_transfer);
20.    };
21. };
```

Code Listing 7. The unmapped code.

```
9.
10.  extend ahb_monitor{
11.    cover transfer_finished is{
12.       item hburst: current_transfer.hburst;
13.       item hsize : current_transfer.hsize;
14.       // More AHB coverage
15.    };
      };
```

Code Listing 8. ahb-monitor.e.

```
   extend ahb_monitor{
16.   !scoreboard: ahb_scoreboard;
17.
18.   on transfer_finished{
19.     scoreboard.add_transfer(current_transfer);
20.   };
21. };
```

Code Listing 9. The unmapped code.

Applying the algorithm to the remaining code creates an aspect list of [AHB], [Monitor], and [Scoreboard]. This means that the code will be placed in ahb-monitor-scoreboard.e.

```
   extend ahb_monitor{
16.   !scoreboard: ahb_scoreboard;
17.
18.   on transfer_finished{
19.     scoreboard.add_transfer(current_transfer);
20.   };
21. };
```

Code Listing 10. The unmapped code.

It's worth returning to the decision we made about the functional coverage code. Because it belongs to a conceptual aspect, one we've decided we don't care about, you might think it could go anywhere, and perhaps we should have just continued with step 1 when we got to line 16. The reason I didn't continue is that I don't like having code unrelated to a physical aspect in an aspect file. If we had kept going with step 1, the functional coverage code would have ended up in ahb-monitor-scoreboard.e, which would have made it really difficult to find. By putting it into the basic "class" aspect (ahb-monitor.e), it is slightly easier to find, because a class is just a catch-all aspect — just like it is an OOP.

4

Creating Flexible Code

But the piece of paper on my desk doesn't have discrete methods. If I decide for example, to burn it for fuel, or fold it into a paper airplane, does that mean that there is a "burn" or "fly" operation that's somehow built into the paper, and that it inherits these operations from a superclass of "flat things"? Nonsense. There are an almost infinite number of things I can do with a simple piece of paper, none of which may have been anticipated by the creator of that paper.

Talin [15]

So what is "flexible code?" Well, it's simply code that can be added to by the end user to augment or change its behavior. It's code that gives the end user some entry points to let them add their own code to the verification environment. By allowing users to augment your code at defined places, you neatly avoid the problems of trying to predict everything that the user might want to do with your code, of failing to do so, and of coding up what you did manage to predict.

You might say that you can predict everything the user wants to do with the code, or that you, the original author, should define exactly what they are allowed to do with it. Let me give you an example of why this is the wrong approach. Imagine you are writing an eVC to stimulate and check the AHB bus protocol. It will probably take a significant amount of effort to get it working, then working with multiple instances in the same design, then debugged and tested on a few example designs, then documented, and then polished for reuse. You take your work of art, place it on your company's IP repository, and wait for the adulation to come rolling in from the happy users. You've thought of everything they would ever want to do — AHB is a standard after all — and locked it down so that the users can't change anything. You're the developer, and you know best.

Unfortunately, the first project team to use it develop smart cards, and they encrypt the address bus for security reasons. Although they've broken the specification a bit, they'd still like to use your code. After all, everything else is the same and they don't see why they should have to duplicate your efforts. They can't, however, without more effort from you. At the same time, one of the major SoC projects tries to use it, but they have a custom security mechanism that says certain bus addresses cannot be accessed without a side-band signal also being asserted. Yet another project tries to use it but they've decided to change the meaning of the HPROT control bits for their design.

I'd like to say this was all invented, but these are all changes to the AHB specification I've encountered at just one client. No matter how much you like to think that you're dealing with a standard and that you know best, the end users will think of something different they want to do. There are more of them, and they're applying more brain power to it than you are.

Note that flexible code is different from configurable code. Configurable code has some built-in switches that let you change how it operates, but only in predefined ways. That means that you have to predict what the options are and code them all. Flexible code pushes this work onto the end user.

Now some of you are probably wondering why I'm even talking about this in an AOP book. You might be saying, "But I can do that in OOP using hooks or callbacks" (essentially two names for the same thing). You are correct — you can do this in OOP, which brings me to the advantage of using AOP for this — it lets you *easily* create flexible code. Creating flexible code in AOP is easy because AOP lets you add advice. It's built right into the language, so it essentially requires no effort. If the code author has followed the guidelines in this book, then you'll have plenty of places in the code to hook into and modify the behavior. If the author hasn't done this, you are limited to the start and end of each method; but still, adding modifications is easy even if your choices of locations are limited.

To do this in OOP is more complex and requires the use of virtual methods and inheritance. In the most basic of cases, a class (let's call it class Foo) declares a number of virtual methods that are the hooks into the class's operation. The user of class Foo creates a new class type which is inherited from class Foo and provides concrete implementations for the hooks he or she wants to use. As long as he or she instantiates the new class instead of class Foo in the verification environment, then the new functionality will be used. It's not always possible to change the classes that are actually used, so a more robust way is sometimes used.

A *functor* is a method that is wrapped in a class. Put it another way, a functor is a class that contains a single method. These form the basis of the more robust OOP hook mechanism. Let's take class Foo again, and let's say that the author of the class wanted to put a hook into one of its methods. To do this, he or she creates a functor base class which defines a type and a virtual method prototype. At the appropriate hook point, he or she puts a pointer to the functor and calls its method. If the user of class Foo would rather have their code called there, then he or she needs to create a concrete functor which inherits from the base functor and creates a concrete version of the method. When an object of class Foo is created, its pointer to the functor is set to an instance of the concrete functor class (which must be created by the user and possibly initialized with a back pointer to the instance of class Foo). Now when the hook is called, it is the concrete functor's method that is called.

If none of that makes any sense to you, then you might appreciate why the AOP solution is easier. If it does make sense to you, then you might appreciate AOP's simplicity for another reason. It requires much less code and initialization.[19] A hook method using functors requires a unique base class for every hook method (if the hook method prototypes are different), a concrete class for every hook method, the instantiation and initialization of the concrete functor, and the initialization of the class Foo objects with the concrete functors.

You can minimize the overhead slightly by creating a class that has multiple hook methods in it. This class is identical to a functor, except that it no longer contains a single method. For want of a better name, I'll call it a hook class. Using this approach, you could create a single hook class for each class in your verification environment that had hooks. For example, you might have `monitor_hook_class`, `bfm_hook_class`, `scoreboard_hook_class`, etc. The advantage of this over functors is that you require fewer classes. The downside is that you have less control over the hooks that you include in your verification environment. If your hook class has hook methods `foo()` and `bar()`, then you cannot include `foo()` without `bar()` and vice versa.

_____

[19] If you are a project manager, then you might appreciate the fact that your team will now be spending much more time verifying the design and less time with language-induced overhead.

This approach also requires the author of class Foo to insert the hook methods. If he or she doesn't, then there's nothing you can do retrospectively to change the operation of the code, unless you can intrusively modify it. With AOP and the first OOP solution you can at least hook into the start and end of the methods (assuming that they are declared as virtual in OOP and you can change the type used).

```
<'
struct example_of_a_hook_s{
  // A basic hook method
  //
  hook() is empty;

  my_method() is{
    outf("Doing some important stuff\n");
    hook();
    outf("Doing more important stuff\n");
  };
};
'>
```

Code Listing 11. A very basic hook method.

If this code was run, the output would be

```
Doing some important stuff
Doing more important stuff
```

To use this hook, the user just needs to add the following code to the project:

```
<'
extend example_of_a_hook_s{
  hook() is also{
    outf("Doing some user defined stuff\n");
  };
};
'>
```

If this code was run, the output would be

```
Doing some important stuff
Doing some user defined stuff
Doing more important stuff
```

Now more complex hooks could pass data in as parameters, but the basic operation doesn't change. You call an empty method, and the user adds advice to it.

The preceding hook is pretty simple, and it provides a single entry point into the flow of execution. Now it could be that there are a number of things that someone might want to do at this entry point. One way of performing multiple tasks here is to extend the hook many times, each time to do something different. For example,

```
A file with one hook extension
<'
extend example_of_a_hook_s{
  hook() is also{
    outf("Doing some user defined stuff (1)\n");
  };
};
'>

A file with another hook extension
<'
extend example_of_a_hook_s{
  hook() is also{
    outf("Doing some user defined stuff (2)\n");
  };
};
'>
```

If this code was run, the output would be

```
Doing some important stuff
Doing some user defined stuff (1)
Doing some user defined stuff (2)
Doing more important stuff
```

However, this depends on the order in which the hook extensions are loaded, so you might end up with

```
Doing some important stuff
Doing some user defined stuff (2)
Doing some user defined stuff (1)
Doing more important stuff
```

This is not a good situation to be in. It can be avoided though by building a *sequencer*. A sequencer is a set of hook methods that are called in a defined order (sequence). You then use advice to extend these hooks, and the call order is ensured. This is something you can do as the author of the code, assuming you know what hooks the users will want, or it can be done by the users themselves. Of course, people could then extend the hooks in the sequencers and end up in the same situation, but you can't solve everything. They can add their own sequencers if required.

If you are writing the original code — that is, you are inserting the hooks in the first place — then you could just call the hooks separately:

```
<'
struct example_of_a_hook_s{

  // Declare the hook methods for the sequencer
  //
  hook_1() is empty;
  hook_2() is empty;

  my_method() is{
    outf("Doing some important stuff\n");
    hook_1();
    hook_2();
    outf("Doing more important stuff\n");
  };
};
'>
```

If you are a user of the code and you want to insert your own sequencer, then you can do this by building it into the original hook method. Imagine you are starting with the code in Code Listing 11:

```
<'
extend example_of_a_hook_s{

  // Declare the hook methods for your sequencer
  //
  my_hook_1() is empty;
  my_hook_2() is empty;

  // Build your sequencer into the original hook
  //
  hook() is also{
    outf("Starting my custom sequencer\n");
    my_hook_1();
    my_hook_2();
    outf("Finishing my custom sequencer\n");
  };
};
'>
```

The user would then add the hook functionality by extending the hooks they just added to the sequencer:

```
A file with one hook extension
<'
extend example_of_a_hook_s{
  my_hook_1() is also{
    outf("Doing some user defined stuff (1)\n");
  };
};
'>

A file with another hook extension
<'
extend example_of_a_hook_s{
```

```
  my_hook_2() is also{
     outf("Doing some user defined stuff (2)\n");
  };
};
'>
```

If this code was run, the output would be

```
Doing some important stuff
Starting my custom sequencer
Doing some user defined stuff (1)
Doing some user defined stuff (2)
Finishing my custom sequencer
Doing more important stuff
```

The user defined hooks are *always* called in this order. Not only does it solve the problem of the call order changing, but by giving the hooks meaningful names, you can create a programming interface that should make the code easier to understand.

One further enhancement you can make to sequencers is to encapsulate them in a class so that you can reuse them elsewhere. The advantage of a class-based sequencer is that it can be added to multiple methods from multiple classes, which might be something you require. For example, you could add the same sequencer to all monitors in your verification environment so that the user can have the same chances to customize a transaction before its existence is reported to the rest of the verification environment.

```
A file with the reusable sequencer
<'
struct my_sequencer_s{
  hook_1() is empty;
  hook_2() is empty;
```

```
  // Call this from your code to initiate the
  // sequencer
  //
  execute_sequencer() is{
    hook_1();
    hook_2();
  };
};
'>


A file that uses the reusable sequencer
<'
struct a_struct_that_needs_a_sequencer_s{
  my_method() is{
    outf("Doing some important stuff\n");

    var sequencer: sequencer_s = new;

    // You might need to initialize the sequencer
    // with some data for it to operate on
    //
    sequencer.execute_sequencer();

    outf("Doing more important stuff\n");
  };
};
'>
```

This approach does require more effort to set up, but it then means you can use the sequencer elsewhere:

```
Another file that uses the reusable sequencer
<'
struct another_struct_that_needs_a_sequencer_s{
  my_method() is{
    outf("Stuff from another struct\n");

    var sequencer: sequencer_s = new;
```

```
        // You might need to initialize the sequencer
        // with some data for it to operate on operate on
        //
        sequencer.execute_sequencer();


        outf("Other stuff from another struct\n");
    };
};
'>
```

A real example of sequencers in action would probably be useful about now. Imagine your verification environment has a scoreboard that looks like Code Listing 12 (although in a real design it would probably be spread over a few files):

```
<'
// Specify the kinds of transaction we can have. IDLE
// means the bus is doing nothing. Everything else
// relates to the transaction's position in the burst
//
type transaction_kind_t: [FIRST, MIDDLE, LAST, IDLE];


// The transaction struct
//
struct transaction_s{
 address : uint;
 data    : uint;
 kind    : transaction_kind_t;


 // Should we ignore the transaction? Set to TRUE if
 // the scoreboard should ignore it.
 //
 !ignore : bool;
```

```
 init() is also{
    ignore = FALSE;
 };
};


// Specifies the kinds of scoreboard we can have
//
type scoreboard_kind_t: [BUS, BRIDGE];


// A simplified scoreboard. Only the bits that
// are relevant to this example are shown.
//
struct scoreboard_s{
 kind                   : scoreboard_kind_t;
 !primary_transactions  : list of transaction_s;
 !secondary_transactions : list of transaction_s;

 // Call this to add a primary side transaction
 // to the scoreboard
 //
 add_primary_transaction(t: transaction_s) is{
   if(t.ignore == FALSE){
     primary_transactions.add(t);
   };
 };

 // Call this to add a secondary side transaction to
 // the scoreboard
 //
 add_secondary_transaction(t: transaction_s) is{
   if(t.ignore == FALSE){
     secondary_transactions.add(t);
   };
 };
};
'>
```

Code Listing 12. The scoreboard for the sequencer example.

Let's say there are three things that you want to do before adding a transaction to the scoreboard. You want to check whether it should be added at all, you want to mutate the transaction, and you want to display the transaction. The order of these is important. There is no point displaying the transaction before it is mutated, or mutating it if it's going to be rejected.

The original author didn't add any hooks for you to do this, but that's not a problem for you. Although there are no explicit hooks, AOP has them built in, so you can extend the `add_primary_transaction()` and `add_secondary_transaction()` methods yourself. By using `is first` advice, you can ensure that you can modify the transactions before the scoreboard does anything with them. If you don't use a sequencer, then you'll have to ensure that the advice is declared in the correct order so that it is loaded, and executed, in the correct order. That's not a good way to go, so you decide to take the extra 10 seconds to build a sequencer to make sure that your three hook methods are always called in the correct order. In fact, because you want to add the sequencer to two methods (and maybe more if you have other scoreboards in your verification environment), you decide that another 20 seconds building a class-based sequencer is a good idea.

```
A file that contains the sequencer that you'll add to
your scoreboards
<'
type scoreboard_side_t: [PRIMARY, SECONDARY];

// The sequencer that calls three hook methods for
// the operations we predict that a user would like
// to do
//
struct scoreboard_add_transaction_sequencer_s{
```

```
    scoreboard_kind: scoreboard_kind_t;
    scoreboard_side: scoreboard_side_t;

    mutate_transaction (t: transaction_s) is empty;
    display_transaction(t: transaction_s) is empty;
    check_transaction  (t: transaction_s) is empty;

    execute(t: transaction_s) is{
      check_transaction  (t);
      mutate_transaction (t);
      display_transaction(t);
    };
};
'>


A file that adds the sequencer to your scoreboard_s
class
<'
// Add the sequencer to the add_*_transaction()
// methods
//
extend scoreboard_s{
  add_primary_transaction(t: transaction_s) is first{
    var s:= new scoreboard_sequencer_s with{
                  .scoreboard_kind = kind;
                  .scoreboard_side = PRIMARY;
    };
    s.execute(t);
  };

  add_secondary_transaction(t: transaction_s) is first{
    var s: = new scoreboard_sequencer_s with{
                  .scoreboard_kind = kind;
                  .scoreboard_side = SECONDARY;
    };
    s.execute(t);
  };
};
'>
```

All you have to do now is extend these hook methods with the checking, mutating, and displaying code that you wanted to add. The following code shows how the sequencer can be used to customize the operation of the scoreboard and how the hooks can be extended for all scoreboards or just for one side of a particular type of scoreboard. In a real verification environment, the peripheral names could also be included as determinants to further control the customization granularity.

```
<'
// Extend the hooks in the scoreboard sequencer
// to apply project-specific behavior
//

// Globally extend the check_transaction() hook
// to reject IDLE transactions
//
extend scoreboard_sequencer_s{
  check_transaction(t: transaction_s) is also{
    if(t.kind == IDLE){
      t.ignore = TRUE;
    };
  };
};

// Globally extend the display_transaction()
// hook to show the transaction being added
//
extend scoreboard_sequencer_s{
  display_transaction(t: transaction_s) is also{
    if(t.ignore == TRUE) { return; };
    out("Adding a transaction to the ",
        scoreboard_side, " side of a ",
        scoreboard_kind, " scoreboard");
    print t using radix = HEX;
  };
};
```

```
// Extend the mutate_transaction() hook, but
// only for the secondary side of bridges. This
// is to do a bit of address remapping, which
// makes the core comparison method generic to
// all types of scoreboard
//
extend BRIDGE SECONDARY scoreboard_sequencer_s{
  !offset: uint;
  mutate_transaction (t: transaction_s) is also{
    t.address += offset;
  };
};
'>
```

The following code fragments are templates to help you get started creating sequencers. The first is for in-line sequencers, and the second is for a class-based sequencer.

```
// This is a template for a sequencer. It shows
// the basic operation of a sequencer, and it's
// intended to provide a starting point for
// implementing a real sequencer in your
// verification environment.
//
struct class_that_needs_a_sequencer_s{

  // This is the method you want to add advice
  // to. The advice must get called in the
  // correct order after the root method has
  // completed
  //
  my_method() is{};

  // Declare the sequencer hooks. Note that in
  // your verification environment, you might
```

```
// want to pass parameters into these. Just
// change the prototypes to do so. Also, try
// to think of better names
//
sequencer_hook_1() is empty;
sequencer_hook_2() is empty;
sequencer_hook_3() is empty;

// Create the sequencer and add it to the end
// of the root method
//
my_method() is also{
  sequencer_hook_1();
  sequencer_hook_2();
  sequencer_hook_3();
};
};
'>
```

Code Listing 13. Template for a basic sequencer.

```
// This is a template for a sequencer. It shows
// the basic operation of a sequencer, and it's
// intended to provide a starting point for
// implementing a real sequencer in your
// verification environment.
//
struct class_that_needs_a_sequencer_s{

  // This is the method you want to add advice
  // to. The advice must get called in the
  // correct order after the root method has
  // completed
  //
  my_method() is{};
};

struct sequencer_template_s{
```

```
// Declare the sequencer hooks. Note that in
// your verification environment, you might
// want to pass parameters into these. Just
// change the prototypes to do so. Also, try
// to think of better names
//
sequencer_hook_1() is empty;
sequencer_hook_2() is empty;
sequencer_hook_3() is empty;

execute() is{
  sequencer_hook_1();
  sequencer_hook_2();
  sequencer_hook_3();
};
};

extend class_that_needs_a_sequencer_s{

// Create the sequencer and add it to the end
// of the root method
//
my_method() is also{
  var sequencer: sequencer_s = new;

  // You might need to initialize the
  // sequencer with some data for it to
  // operate on
  //
  sequencer.execute();
};
};
'>
```

Code Listing 14. Template for a class-based sequencer.

Now that you know how to create hooks and sequencers, your only remaining job is to make sure that you insert enough for the end users to use. If you know that certain extensions will be needed, such as in the previous scoreboard example, then you can add the appropriate hooks when you write the code. What if you don't know what hooks are needed?

Well, accepted good coding practice says you should compose your code using many small methods [16]. Quite how small you want to make these methods is a matter of personal taste, but the point is that if you have a method in AOP, you get a hook for free. Therefore, by breaking large methods down into a collection of smaller methods, you not only gain some standard programming benefits, but your users also get a whole bunch of hooks for free.

5

Creating Pluggable Code

Pluggable code is code that can be nonintrusively plugged into your verification environment or unplugged from your verification environment, just by including (or not) the appropriate files. Think about it as self-connecting or self-integrating code. Pluggable code allows you to add a new feature to your verification environment simply by including it in the manifest file or to remove a feature simply by excluding the file.

Why would you want this? One reason might be to expand or reduce the number of packet types that can be randomly selected during a simulation run. By selecting which files are included in the load phase, you can control what packets your tests can randomly chose from. For instance, you might normally exclude the file that contains the packet that contains errors, but for particular tests, you might decide that that is the *only* packet type you want to test. Or perhaps some packets take a long time to process, so you normally want to exclude them unless you are running simulations overnight.

A second reason for creating pluggable code might be resource management. For example, if your verification environment is to support an SoC that can have a USB or an SDIO host interface, then making these pluggable means that only one has to be compiled into your verification environment. Not only will this speed up the compilation process, but it will also mean that your simulation of an SDIO-based SoC doesn't consume a license for the USB eVC that you have bought.

A third reason might be to control the log file trace for a particular simulation. You can create different aspects that trace different information from different components in the design and verification environment and just plug the appropriate ones in for your simulation. "Debugging using AOP" on page 204 looks at this idea more.

Now the idea that you can control the structure and content of your verification environment by selectively including files might sound like a bad idea to some people, but in reality it's no different from using `#defines` or `'defines` to do the same task. It's very common in software design to have conditionally compiled code. The advantages with AOP are that you don't have to scatter the control flags throughout your code, you can isolate and examine the code for each configuration, and you can add new configurations later — you don't have to build everything in up front.

Creating pluggable code requires a simple three-step process.

1. Encapsulate the pluggable code as an aspect.

2. Write the code that connects the pluggable code to the verification environment. Encapsulate the code in the appropriate aspects.

3. Write a manifest file just for your feature.

Step 1 is covered in detail in "What aspects do I want to use?" on page 70. This step ensures that each feature that you want to make pluggable is encapsulated in its own aspect.

Step 2 is partially covered in "Mapping aspects to files" on page 75, because it tells you how to encapsulate the infrastructure code in its own files so that your pluggable features remain independent from the verification environment (and therefore, reusable in other verification environments). This is optional of course, but it makes your code much more reusable at a cost of having one or two more files. There are some details in step 2 that I'll come back to shortly.

The separation of the pluggable code from the verification environment, and from other pluggable code, is essential because you will include or exclude features by including or excluding their files, so all pluggable features have to exist in isolation. If any code for feature Foo exists in files that contain code for feature Bar, then Foo and Bar can only be plugged (or unplugged) together.

Step 3 is to create a manifest file for your pluggable feature (Figure 5.1). This simplifies the top-level manifest file, because you only need to include or exclude one file to include or exclude a feature. In fact, you should have two manifest files for your pluggable feature. The first will just contain the files required for the core feature itself and can be reused in other verification environments, if required.

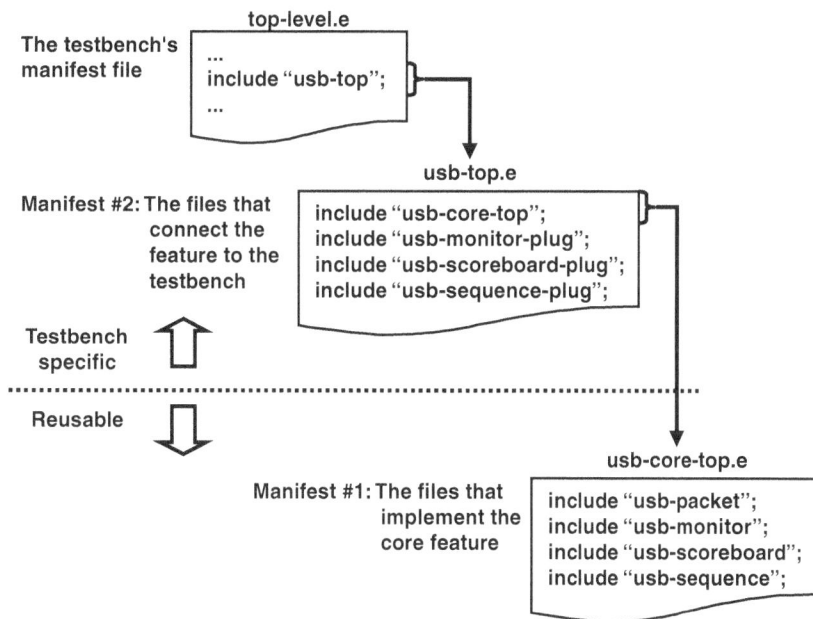

Figure 5.1 The manifest files for a pluggable feature.

The second manifest file that you should create will contain the first manifest file (the one with the feature's core files) and all of the files required to plug the feature into your particular verification environment. It is this manifest file that your top-level manifest file will include.

The description of step 2 above glossed over the important detail of connecting the code to the verification environment. Exactly *how* do you connect pluggable code to the verification environment? Well that depends on a couple of things:

1. Can the verification environment interact with the pluggable feature? That is, does the verification environment know about, and interact with, the feature even though it doesn't know which variation is present?

2. If the verification environment can interact with a pluggable feature, can it select between different variations of the feature? For example, if the verification environment interacts with packets (the feature), can it select between a data packet and a control packet (the feature's variations)?

If the verification environment does not interact with the pluggable feature, then life is easy. The pluggable feature can probe into the verification environment as needed to get access to the information it needs, and you can have multiple feature variations present at the same time. For example, you might have several variations on a scoreboard that passively connect themselves to the verification environment and all operate at the same time. In this case, connecting to the verification environment might just be extending a class and adding an "is also" extension to an existing method. The following code is an example of pluggable code that probes into the verification environment and connects itself. The monitor is extended and the scoreboard added, all without the existing verification environment becoming aware of the scoreboard.

```
// Extend the monitor to add the link to the
// scoreboard
//
extend ahb_monitor{
  !scoreboard: ahb_scoreboard;

  on transfer_finished{
    scoreboard.add_transfer(current_transfer);
  };
};
```

Code Listing 15. An example of a probe.

If the verification environment does need to interact with the pluggable feature, then you'll have to provide the verification environment with some sort of "*socket*" for the feature to plug into. I call the pluggable feature a *plug*. This socket[20] is simply a way for the verification environment to interact with something that it doesn't know the exact details of, and will either be a handle to a base class, or a method that it can call. In the latter case, the socket is simply a method prototype (declared as "is empty") and each variation of the feature has to provide a body for the method (declared as "is also").

Code Listing 16 shows an example of a *method socket*. It shows a struct that is used to model an ALU operation and provides a method called `calculate()`, which the verification environment calls to get the result of a particular operation. Although the verification environment (well, at least the ALU model) knows that there are models of different ALU operations and it can call `calculate()` to get the result for a particular operation, it doesn't actually know which operations are supported by the ALU.

---

[20] You'll soon notice that a "socket" looks suspiciously similar to a hook. They are really the same thing, but I use socket to show that the *intent* is to create pluggable code. A hook "allows" the user to add functionality if they want to, but a socket "mandates" a plug. Also, a socket can be a handle to a base class, whereas a hook in AOP is seldom done this way (why bother?).

```
type operation_t : [];
unit alu_model_u{

  // "current_operation" is used as a
  // determinant.
  // Each operation extends this class and
  // provides a body for calculate().
  //
  current_operation: operation_t;
  calculate(a: int, b: int): int is undefined;
};

// Add a new operation to the model
//
extend operation_t : [ADD];
extend ADD alu_model_u{
  calculate(a: int, b: int): int is{
    result = a + b;
  };
};

// Add a new operation to the model
//
extend operation_t : [MUL];
extend MUL alu_model_u{
  calculate(a: int, b: int): int is{
    result = a * b;
  };
};
```

Code Listing 16. An example of a method socket.

If the socket is a handle to a base class (a *class socket*), then the pluggable code will be a concrete version of the class (either like- or when-inherited from the base class), and the concrete classes will have to provide an implementation for the methods that the verification environment will call.

The following code shows an example of a class socket. In fact, it is just a slight variation on the previous example. There, the new operations are added directly to the ALU model using when-inheritance. The operations are modeled as separate classes, and the model just contains a handle to the active operation.

```
type operation_t : [];
unit alu_model_u{

  // "current_operation" is NOT used as a
  // determinant. Instead, it is a handle to
  // a base class that provides a calculation
  // result. To model new operations, create a
  // concrete class for the operation,
  // instantiate it, and set current_operation
  // equal to it.
  //
  current_operation: alu_operation_s;

  get_result(a: int, b: int): int is{
    result = current_operation.calculate(a, b);
  };
};

struct alu_operation_s{
  kind: operation_t;
  calculate(a: int, b: int): int is undefined;
};

// Create a new operation for the model
//
extend operation_t : [ADD];
extend ADD alu_operation{
  calculate(a: int, b: int): int is{
    result = a + b;
  };
};
```

```
// Create a new operation for the model
//
extend operation_t : [MUL];
extend MUL alu_operation{
  calculate(a: int, b: int): int is{
    result = a * b;
  };
};
```

If the verification environment can interact with the plug-gable feature, then you'll need to consider if the verification environment can select which variation to use. If you can only have one variation included in a simulation run, then you can initialize the socket manually by including the correct files at compile time. If the socket is a method call, then this is the only approach that you can use. If the plug-gable feature can be selected at runtime, then you'll need to use some code to initialize the socket correctly. This requires a factory, and I'll tell you about that soon. Before that, though, it's worth getting to know the extendable case statement.

5.1 The extendable case statement

Pluggable code is a great thing, but it relies on being able to nonintrusively add or remove code from the verification environment. Conditional statements, such as case statements or if-then-else statements, can cause problems with this because their branches tend to be hardwired, stopping you from plug-ging and unplugging features. If you unplug feature Foo, then you need to remove any conditional branches that select feature Foo. If you want to plug in feature Bar, then you'll need to add conditional branches to deal with Bar. For case statement this can be done in AOP and OOP[21] with some forethought. Unfortunately, this approach cannot replace an if-then-else statement. These have an execution priority, and as I discussed in "Controlling the order of method extension calls" on page 65, it is very difficult to control the order in which "is also" extensions are called.

The obvious solution to this problem is to create a case statement that has dynamic branches. Dynamic branches might sound complex, but in reality, they are simply hooks. In fact, each dynamic case statement consists of some infrastructure, one hook, and a number of user-supplied implementations of the hook. Each implementation is a dynamic branch. To create a dynamic case statement, simply define a method that you call where you would have the case statement, and inside this method call an (initially) empty hook method. For each branch of the case statement, add an `is also` advice to the hook method.

The following code shows one sample configuration for an extendable case, but there are other possibilities. You can change the method names, the branch selector, the return type (if any), the struct the method is declared in, and the default branch behavior. These are discussed in more detail in the in-line comments. Code Listing 17 is a template for the extendable case, Code Listing 18 is a template for a branch, and Code Listing 19 shows how you would use this extendable case.

```
<'
// This type is used to select the correct case
// statement branch. The extendable case
```

---

[21]The OOP solution requires more effort because it needs you to declare and set up a Functor (see Chapter 4) for each branch.

```
// statement could also use a raw number,
// such as an int or a uint, or it could
// use a combination of parameters to select a
// branch.
//
type branch_selector_t: [];

// This struct holds the extendable case
// statement, but there is no need to have
// it in a special class at all. You can
// just declare the do_case and branch hook
// methods in the struct where they will be
// used if that is more convenient.
//
// In this example, the branch performs an
// action and returns a pass/fail flag. In
// your example, it could return a struct
// or even return nothing.
//
struct extendable_case_s{

  // This is the hook method that will be
  // extended to implement each "branch" of
  // the case statement. Feel free to change
  // the name in your own implementation.
  //
  branch_hook(id     : branch_selector_t,
              handled: *bool) : bool is empty;

  // Call this method to execute the case
  // statement. Feel free to change the name
  // in your own implementation.
  //
  do_case(id: branch_selector_t): bool is {

    // The "handled" variable is passed to each
    // branch. If they accept the ID and
    // execute, they should set it to TRUE.
    // If "handled" is still FALSE by the time
    // branch_hook() returns, it means no
```

```
    // branch has been selected and the default
    // action should occur. In this case it is
    // to print an error, but some other
    // default behavior could be implemented
    // instead.
    //
    var handled: bool = FALSE;


    result = branch_hook(id, handled);


    // The "default" branch. You can change the
    // behavior to something more appropriate
    // for you.
    //
    if(handled == FALSE){
      error("\n",
        ".---(extendable_case error)-------\n",
        "| No branch claimed ID ", id,      "\n",
        "| I cannot continue until this is
          fixed\n",
        "`-------------------------------\n");
    };
  };
};
'>
```

Code Listing 17. A template for an extendable case.

```
<'
// Define a branch identifier
//
extend branch_selector_t: [BRANCH_1];

extend extendable_case_s{

  // Add a "branch" into the extendable case
  // statement
```

```
  //
  branch_hook(id      : branch_selector_t,
              handled: *bool) : bool is also{

    if(handled == FALSE and id == BRANCH_1){
      message(LOW, "Executing BRANCH_1");

      // Do some interesting stuff that only
      // BRANCH_1 can do.
      handled = TRUE;
      result  = TRUE; // ok, this passed
    };
  };
};
'>
```

Code Listing 18. A branch template for an extendable case.

```
<'
extend sys{
  run() is also{
    var my_case        : extendable_case_s = new;
    var passed         : bool;
    var branch_selector: branch_selector_t;

    // Pass the extendable case a randomized
    // branch selector and capture the
    // pass/fail result
    //
    gen branch_selector;
    passed = my_case.do_case(branch_selector);
  };
};
'>
```

Code Listing 19. Using the extendable case.

Consider the case where you have a set of register definitions,[22] of base type `register_s`. Each of these register objects has a unique name. To provide an API to the test writer, you create a method called `get_register()`. This takes the register name as a parameter and returns the correct register. Here is a very small example to show this:

```
<'
// This type holds the names of all registers
//
type register_names_t: [STATUS, ID];

// This struct is the basic register struct.
// You will have one instance of this per
// register name.
//
struct register_s{
  name: register_names_t;

  // This struct should be extended for each
  // register type to store its fields, access
  // masks, etc.
};

extend ID register_s{
  // Define some fields for the ID register
};

extend STATUS register_s{
  // Define some fields for the STATUS register
};
```

---

[22] This way of defining registers makes a nice example for an extendable case statement, but is not a good way to define registers in general. It doesn't easily allow you to instantiate multiple instances of the same register or loop through the registers.

```
// This holds all of the registers, and
// provides a simple API to get a register
// by name and to display all registers
//
struct registers_s{
  id_reg    : ID      register_s;
  status_reg: STATUS register_s;

  // Call this method to get the "name"
  // register
  //
  get_register(name: register_names_t):
  register_s is {
     case(name){
       ID: {
         result = id_reg;
       };
       STATUS: {
         result = status_reg;
       };
     };
  };

  // Call this to display all registers
  display() is {
    print get_register(ID);
    print get_register(STATUS);
  };
};

extend registers_s{
  registers: registers_s;

  run() is also{
    registers.display();
  };
};
'>
```

Code Listing 20. Example of a nonextendable case statement.

This solution works well, right up until the point where you add a new register type. For instance, the aspect to add a CONTROL register is shown in Code Listing 21. Notice that the one thing that is missing is the extension to `get_register()`. Because it was written in a nonextendable manner, you will have to intrusively edit the original `get_register()` definition to add the extra branch in the case statement. In this particular example that would be difficult, because the CONTROL register name would have to be declared before the `get_register()` method, which would further remove the advantages of AOP.

```
<'
extend register_names_t: [CONTROL];
struct CONTROL register_s{
  // Define some fields for the CONTROL register
};

extend registers_s{

  // Instantiate the control register
  //
  control_reg: CONTROL register_s;

  display() is also{
    print get_register(CONTROL);
  };
};
'>
```

Code Listing 21. The CONTROL register aspect—this doesn't work with a nonextendable case statement.

If `get_register()` had been written using an extendable case statement, then the CONTROL register aspect could be fully encapsulated.

The following code shows what the preceding example looks like when an extendable case statement is used. Note that all registers can be fully encapsulated in aspects, and registers can be added or removed without intrusively modifying any existing code.

```
<'
// This type holds the names of all registers
//
type register_names_t: [];


// This struct is the basic register struct.
// You will have one instance of this per
// register name.
//
struct register_s{
  name: register_names_t;


  // This struct should be extended for each
  // register type to store its fields, access
  // masks, etc.
};


// This holds all of the registers, and
// provides a simple API to get a register
// by name and to display all registers
//
struct registers_s{
  get_register_hook(name    : register_names_t,
                    handled: *bool):
                            register_s is empty;


  // Call this method to get the "name"
  // register
  //
```

```
    get_register(name: register_names_t):
                                    register_s is{
      var handled: bool = FALSE;
      result = get_register_hook(name, handled);

      if(handled == FALSE){
        error("\n",
          ".---(get_register() error)--------\n",
          "| No one claimed to know about a ",
           name, " register\n",
          "| I cannot continue until this is
           fixed\n",
          "`--------------------------------\n");
      };
    };


  // Call this to display all registers
  //
  display() is empty;
};


extend sys{
  registers: registers_s;


  run() is also{
    registers.display();
  };
};
'>
```

Code Listing 22. The infrastructure for the extendable case statement example.

```
<'
// -----\/----- ID Register aspect-----\/-----
extend register_names_t: [ID];
```

```
extend ID register_s{
  // Define some fields for the ID register
};

extend registers_s{

  // Instantiate the ID register
  //
  id_reg: ID register_s;

  // Add a "branch" into the extendable case
  // statement
  //
  get_register_hook(name    : register_names_t,
                    handled: *bool) is also{
    if(handled == FALSE and name == ID){
      result  = id_reg;
      handled = TRUE;
    };
  };

  display() is also{
    print get_register(ID);
  };
};
// -----/\----- ID Register aspect -----/\-----
'>
```

Code Listing 23. The ID register aspect for the extendable case statement example.

```
<'
// ----\/---- STATUS Register aspect ----\/----
extend register_names_t: [STATUS];
extend STATUS register_s{
  // Define some fields for the STATUS register
};
```

```
extend registers_s{

  // Instantiate the STATUS register
  //
  status_reg: STATUS register_s;


  // Add a "branch" into the extendable case
  // statement
  //
  get_register_hook(name    : register_names_t,
                    handled: *bool):
                                register_s is also{
    if(handled == FALSE and name == STATUS){
      result  = status_reg;
      handled = TRUE;
    };
  };


  display() is also{
    print get_register(STATUS);
  };
};
// ----/\---- STATUS Register aspect ----/\----
'>
```

Code Listing 24. The STATUS register aspect for the extendable case statement example.

```
<'
// ----\/---- CONTROL Register aspect ----\/----
extend register_names_t: [CONTROL];
extend CONTROL register_s{
  // Define some fields for the CONTROL register
};
```

```
extend registers_s{
  // Instantiate the CONTROL register
  //
  control_reg: CONTROL register_s;

  // Add a "branch" into the extendable case
  // statement
  //

  get_register_hook(name    : register_names_t,
                    handled: *bool):
                            register_s is also{
    if(handled == FALSE and name == CONTROL){
      result  = control_reg;
      handled = TRUE;
    };
  };

  display() is also{
    print get_register(CONTROL);
  };
};
// ----/\---- CONTROL Register aspect ----/\----
'>
```

Code Listing 25. The CONTROL register aspect for the extendable case statement example.

5.2   The factory pattern

The extendable case statement is an essential building block when you're writing pluggable code. One place where you'll use it a lot is when you are creating the sockets required for pluggable code that is run-time selectable. Remember from a few pages back that these sockets are just handles to base classes, and the pluggable code is an instance of a concrete class.

Creating a new instance of a class can be a complex business. While calling `new` or `gen` will create the object and set up the default member values, further processing may be required before the object is available for use. For instance, the object may have to be registered in a central database, or some status information about the verification environment must be passed into the object. It could be that the exact nuances of the produced object depend on a query to the coverage database to decide what the most useful type would be. For example, you may want a data packet, but whether it should be a LARGE or SMALL data packet depends on the current coverage situation.

A *factory* is an instance of a class whose sole purpose is to create instances of other classes. You supply the factory with the information that is to be used to create the object, and the factory performs all of the necessary operations and returns the initialized object. The type of the object returned will depend on the information supplied by you. This information can be as simple as a number or a value from an enumerated type. The factory then does all of the work and returns a fully initialized object for you to use. "Creating reusable layered sequences," on page 188, shows how more complex information can be generically passed to the factory.

A factory relies on all of the objects it can create having a common base type, and the object returned is cast to this type. If you need to access the concrete type, then you will have to cast the base object to the concrete object using `as_a()`. Of course, this assumes that you know what type the factory will return, given the data you passed to the factory. If not, then the base class and factory need to be modified so that you can determine the concrete type by looking at fields in the base type. If you use when-inheritance instead of like-inheritance to create your class family, then the information you need is in the determinants.

At the heart of most simple factories is a large case statement that decodes the information passed by the user (the number, enumerated type, etc.) and selects the correct branch to generate the object. This branch can contain any amount of procedural code and can do quite a lot of processing to make sure that the object creation is handled fully. The problem with this approach is scalability — the case statement has to have new branches added if new subtypes are added to the class family. This intrusive modification may be unacceptable in many cases. An extendable case statement can be used to remove this problem.

One common scenario in verification environments is to have a stream of data, such as bytes, that have to be turned into an object representation, such as a packet. The following example shows a factory that takes a stream of bytes and creates either a `data_packet` object or a `control_packet` object. These packet types are pluggable, and the example will show how a new type, a `routing_packet,` can be plugged into the verification environment.

Packets in this example are transported as a stream of bytes. The first byte represents the type of packet and the second byte its length. The third byte, and all subsequent bytes, form the payload, which has a different format for each packet type. To make the packets into a family of classes, and because all packets share some common fields, a base class called `packet_s` is created. Like-inheritance[23] is used to create the `data_packet_s` and `control_packet_s` classes. Each packet class, including the base class, has a

---

[23] Note that when-inheritance could also be used instead to define the packets, with no change in functionality. Like-inheritance has been used to provide consistency with the information you'll find when you read software literature about the factory pattern. In a real testbench, I'd probably use when-inheritance.

`populate()` method that extracts information from the byte stream and initializes member variables with it. Figure 5.2 shows the structure of a factory that doesn't use an extendable case statement.

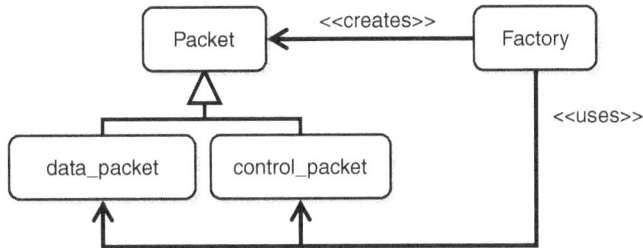

Figure 5.2   The operation of the nonextendable case statement example.

The public interface to the factory is a method called `get_packet()`, which the user passes a list of bytes to. The factory's task is to decode these bytes and to create the correct type of packet. The simplest way to do this is to have a case statement that interrogates the first byte in the stream and instantiates the correct type of object based on its value. As discussed earlier, the problem with this approach is that the addition of new packet types, or the removal of old packet types, requires changes to existing code.

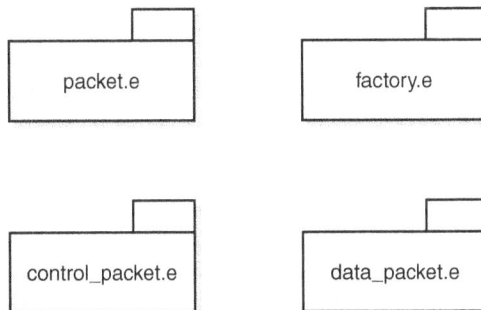

Figure 5.3   The file structure of the nonextendable case.

Figure 5.3 shows the file structure of the classes for the solution that doesn't use an extendable case statement. Imagine that we wanted to add a new packet, called `routing_packet`. This would require modification of the `factory.e` file, which may not be possible or desirable (Figure 5.4).

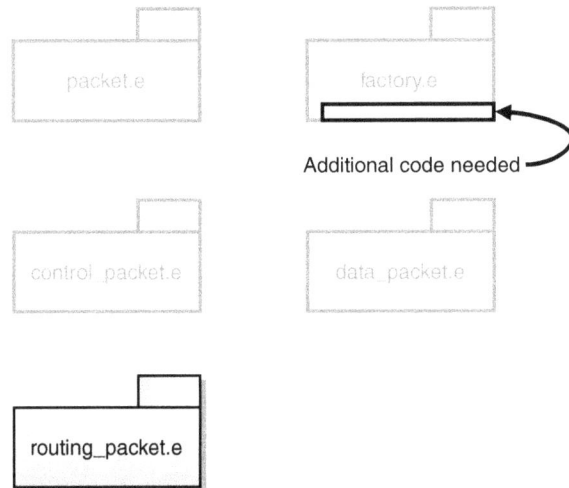

Figure 5.4   Adding a new packet to the factory that doesn't use an extendable case statement.

The extendable case statement approach to the problem changes the structure of the factory. The factory can be easily split into a class and aspects. The class provides the infrastructure for the factory and defines its interfaces. The aspects provide the customizations that create the different classes, such as the `data_packet` and the `control_packet` (Figure 5.5).

The file structure shown in Figure 5.6 is used to deploy the solution. The factory class remains in `factory.e`, and the aspect files are `factory-data_packet.e` and `factory-control_packet.e`.

The advantages the extendable case statement can be clearly seen from this diagram in Figure 5.6. The addition of a new packet, say `routing_packet`, requires no modification

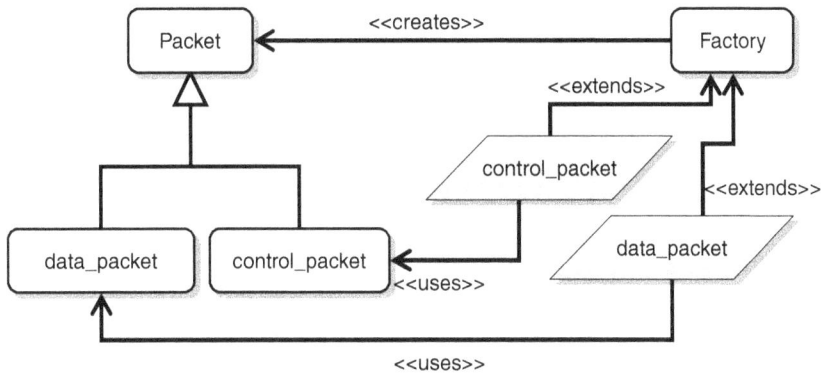

Figure 5.5   The operation of the extendable case statement example.

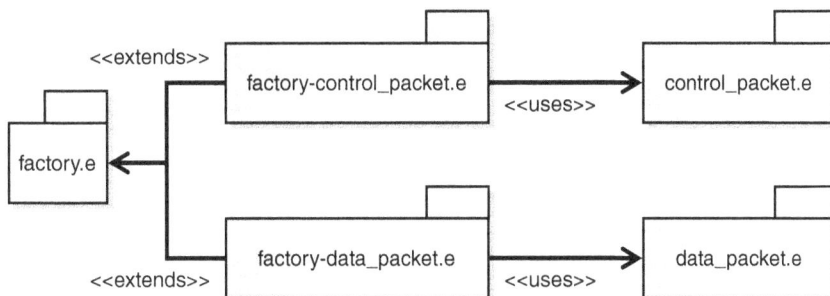

Figure 5.6   The file structure of the extendable case statement example.

of existing files (Figure 5.7). Compare this to Figure 5.4 where existing files did have to be modified.

The following code shows how the factory is coded using the extendable case approach. The first three code listings show how the basic infrastructure for the factory is defined. It is important to note that there is absolutely nothing in any of these files that refers to the different packet types.

■   `packet_types.e`: The basic type definitions needed by the factory. Note that the different types of the packets are not declared here. To do so would mean that the file would have to be modified if one of the packet types was removed.

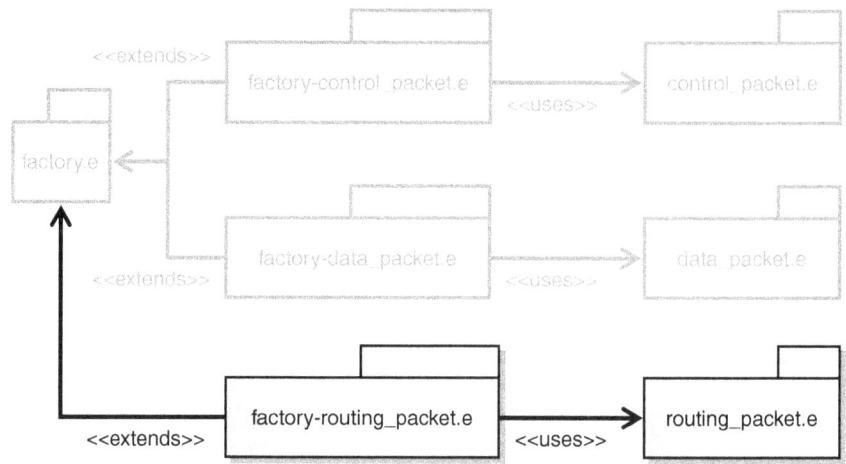

Figure 5.7   Adding a new packet to the factory that uses an extendable case statement.

- packet.e: The packet base class.

- factory.e: The basic factory, implemented using an extendable case statement (see "The extendable case statement" on page 120 for more information).

The following files are used to define the aspects — the packet types — that the factory will deal with. Each aspect requires two files. The first of these defines the packet itself, and the second defines the code that extends the factory to deal with the packet.

- data_packet.e: The definition of the data packet.

- factory-data_packet.e: The extension to the factory so that it can deal with the data packet.

- control_packet.e: The definition of the control packet.

- factory-control_packet.e: The extension to the factory so that it can deal with the control packet.

```
<'
// This type will be extended to hold the names
// of the different packets (concrete
// classes) that the factory can deal with
//
type packet_types_t: [];

// This type just defines byte offsets within
// the byte stream
//
type packet_fields_t:    [TYPE    = 0,
                          LENGTH  = 1,
                          PAYLOAD = 2];

'>
```

Code Listing 26. packet_types.e.

```
<'
// The packet base class. This will be extended
// using like-inheritance purely to make the
// example resemble an OOP factory. If you go
// reading about the factory pattern,
// everything you find will be OOP based, so
// this will help you compare
//
struct packet_s {
  length: byte;
  type  : packet_types_t;

  // This method starts the conversion from a
  // stream of bytes to a concrete object. It
  // decodes some of the information that is
  // common to all packets.
  //
  populate(stream: list of byte) is {

    // Decode the byte that describes the
    // packet type, and store it
    //
    type = stream[packet_fields_t'TYPE.
      as_a(uint)].as_a(packet_types_t);
```

```
    // Decode the byte that describes the
    // packet length, and store it
    //
    length = stream[packet_fields_t'LENGTH.
      as_a(byte)];
  };
};
'>
```

Code Listing 27. packet.e.

```
<'
// This is the core of the factory. AOP will
// be used to extend the create_packet()
// method for each packet type we support
//
struct factory_s{
  // This is the user's interface to the
  // factory. They call this, passing in a
  // list of bytes, and they get an
  // initialized object back that is of the
  // correct type
  //
  get_packet(stream: list of byte): packet_s is{
    var handled: bool = FALSE;
    result = create_packet(stream, handled);

    if handled == FALSE{
      error("Unknown packet type");
    };
  };

create_packet(stream : list of byte,
              handled: *bool): packet_s
                                      is empty;
};
'>
```

Code Listing 28. factory.e.

```
<'
// The data_packet class
extend packet_types_t: [DATA = 0];

struct data_packet_s like packet_s{

  // The payload for this packet
  //
  payload: byte;

  // The populate method is used to build the
  // packet from a stream of bytes
  //
  populate(stream: list of byte) is also{
    payload =
    stream[packet_fields_t'PAYLOAD. as_a(int)];
  };
};
'>
```

Code Listing 29. data_packet.e.

```
<'
// This is the extension to the factory for the
// data packet
//
extend factory_s{
  create_packet(stream : list of byte,
                handled: *bool): packet_s
                                      is also{

    // Is this packet for me?
    //
    if stream[packet_fields_t'TYPE.as_a(int)]
              .as_a(packet_types_t) == DATA{
      var packet: data_packet_s = new;
```

```
        packet.populate(stream);
        result   = packet;
        handled = TRUE;
      };
    };
  };
 '>
```

Code Listing 30. factory-data_packet.e.

```
<'
// The control_packet class
extend packet_types_t: [CONTROL = 1];

struct control_packet_s like packet_s{
  number_of_services: int[1..5];

  // The populate method is used to build the
  // packet from a stream of bytes
  populate(stream: list of byte) is also{
    number_of_services =
      stream[packet_fields_t'PAYLOAD.as_a(int)];
  };
};
'>
```

Code Listing 31. control_packet.e.

```
<'
// This is the extension to the factory for the
// control packet
//
extend factory_s{
  create_packet(stream : list of byte,
                handled: *bool): packet_s
                                      is also{
```

```
    // Is this packet for me?
    //
    if stream[packet_fields_t'TYPE.as_a(int)]
           .as_a(packet_types_t) == CONTROL{
      var packet: control_packet_s = new;
      packet.populate(stream);
      result  = packet;
      handled = TRUE;
    };
  };
};
'>
```

Code Listing 32. factory-control-packet.e.

Now if you want to add a new packet type, such as a routing packet, you just have to define the packet and an extension to the factory. No existing code needs to change.

One point that is worth discussing further is the interface to the factory. Any interface you come up with for the factory will last a long time and will end up being used from many pieces of code. Once your code starts being reused, changing the public interface becomes a very tedious, and sometimes impossible, task.

Because of this, it is a good idea to pass all of your parameters to the factory in a struct. The reason for this is simple — you can extend the struct to add new fields without changing the method prototype and without affecting any of the existing code. By applying safe defaults to any new fields that you add, existing code that uses the factory can remain unchanged.

6
Improving Your Productivity

I can live with the shame if it means I'm more productive.

Joel Spolsky [23]

It's an unfortunate fact of life that some of the projects that you'll work on will be late. Some of them will be very late. Even with the best attempts at planning, deadlines seem to mysteriously pass with no obvious reason why the code wasn't ready. Post mortem reviews might reveal some things that perhaps could have been done better, but it can be a struggle to work out where the time went. In his book "The Mythical Man Month" [24], Fred Brooks asked the question how do projects get to be a year late? His answer was quite simple — one day at a time. In many cases, there is no cataclysmic event that knocked the project off course. Time was simply lost in small and forgettable chunks. Nothing major — an hour here implementing some OOP hooks, an hour there working out how to fix someone else's bug that affected your work. A week waiting for someone else to make a change to their code, then a few hours trying to context switch your mind back to what you had been doing when you had stalled. A month rewriting some code you thought you could reuse, but in fact couldn't because it was inflexible. Three days implementing some functionality in your class in case someone eventually needs it. I'm telling you — sometimes it's like you're being nibbled to death by ducks.

Luckily, AOP can help out here as well.

6.1 Shifting the power

One key difference between OOP and AOP is in the allocation
of power. Not in processing power, or verification power, but
in the power to change and augment the code's behavior. In
the power to actually use the code. With an OOP solution, it's
the code's designer that decides what the user can and cannot
do with the code. As a user of OOP code, if you want to make
some nonintrusive modifications, then you're pretty much
reliant on the designer having built in the mechanisms to
do this. Although you might have some luck inheriting from
existing classes and inserting your new classes into the verification environment, there are enough blocking points with
this approach that I've seldom had satisfactory results. I'm
normally at the mercy of the designer having inserted enough
hooks for me to use. I really don't like being at the mercy of
other people when the risks are mine. Finalizing OOP code
so that it can't be changed requires no effort in OOP. In fact,
many people finalize code by mistake. Forgetting to type
virtual in front of a method or making a base class pointer
private can make it unchangeable. It's making OOP code
flexible that requires the skill and effort.

With an AOP solution, the power to extend code lies with
you, the user. Every method call is a hook by default, and
existing structures can be extended. As an end user, you can
change the behavior of someone else's code without having
to write any new classes, without having to ask their permission, and without having to rely on them letting you do so.
You don't have to pray that the original designer was skilled
enough to make his or her code flexible enough to use. It
requires effort to make AOP code inflexible.

This shift in power and control from the writer to the
user means that there are a number of potential blocking

points and time-wasting situations that simply disappear
when you have AOP. This advantage cuts both ways, of
course. As a user of code, you have the flexibility to mold
code to fit your own verification environment. As a writer of
code, you can now relax and stop worrying that you haven't
added enough functionality or that you might not have written everything correctly. It doesn't really matter if your code
isn't configurable enough, and you don't have to worry about
writing code that's perfect for everyone. By transferring
power to the end user, you're also transferring some of your
work. In fact, when you come to use your own code, you
might get both sets of benefits. You will save time when you
initially write the code, because you will not add superfluous features, and you will save time when you come to use
the code, because it can be easily customized to the task at
hand. You will also have more domain experience at that
point, so any code you write will probably be better than it
would have been if you'd written it in advance.

6.2   Dealing with broken code

It would be nice to imagine that all of the verification environment code in the world was bug free. It's not. When you
consider that in most cases the verification environment is
at least as complex as the actual design itself, then there's no
reason to believe that the verification environment code will
work perfectly. Mistakes happen, and it would be foolish to
ignore this fact. So what do you do when you find that the
code you are using has bugs in it?

The academic answers are that you fix the code or that you
ask the original author to fix the code. Those solutions look
nice on paper, but are not always practical in real life. Why
not? Well,

■ What if you don't have access to the source code? It might be encrypted code;

■ What if you don't have permission to change the source code? It might belong to a central IP department in your company;

■ What if the code is in use on other projects and you're worried that fixing the bug will cause them problems? Changing the source might require a complete regression of all of the other projects as a matter of policy;

■ What if you're too busy to fix the bug properly? You might be able to do something quickly that's good enough for your project, but that might be unacceptable to other people;

■ What if you can't convince the code owner that it is a bug? Although the it's-a-bug–no-it's-a-feature debate is endlessly fascinating, the bottom line is that the "feature" isn't right for your verification environment.

So what's the best way to deal with this? Just patch it and move on. Dealing with a bug like this can cost a lot of time on a project. As long as the patch is documented, someone else can deal with the original code at a suitable time. You might be able to fix the bug by adding a hook that preprocesses or postprocesses some data. In the worst case, you might have to replace entire methods.

Sometimes "officially" fixing a bug is just too much effort. It could be that you don't have time at the moment or that you'll just get involved in a public and political battle with the writer of the original code. It may be the case that the solution you need is not enough to fully fix the original class. AOP allows you to stay focused on the real issues at hand — getting your verification environment to work and finding bugs on your project. Spend some time documenting the fix and send it to the person responsible for the class. It then becomes their problem, not yours.

6.3   Handling workarounds

The time between logging an RTL bug and receiving a fix for it can be substantial. The question is, how do you deal with that in your verification environment? If you run your regressions again then you'll just hit the same bug, and that will ruin your run because the log files will be polluted by errors you already know about, and simulations may end early. It will be difficult to identify new bugs because you will still be getting error messages from the old bug. While you are waiting on the fix, you need to do something to make the old bug disappear.

You could do this by changing the verification environment so that it doesn't generate the stimuli necessary to expose the bug, or to not report the error, or by compensating for the bug somehow so that your checkers pass. The risk, of course, is that you'll forget about these modifications and sign off a design that still has bugs in it.

The easy way to deal with this is to do any of the above, but to do it using aspects to modify the verification environment. The key here is to store the modifications in an aspect called "workarounds," such as ahb-workarounds.e. Because all of the verification environment changes required to deal with RTL bugs are stored in one aspect, they can be reviewed and it becomes difficult to forget about them.

For example, an easy way to switch off error messages is to just comment out the error message. After all, once you've debugged what's going on, the chances are that the file open in front of you contains the error message. What could be easier than just commenting it out?

```
check that src.data == dest.data else
  dut_error("CHECK_BRIDGE_12: Data mismatch
  error");
```

becomes

```
// check that src.data == dest.data else
// dut_error("CHECK_BRIDGE_12: Data mismatch
// error");
```

This works perfectly, and when the next regression is run only new bugs will be reported. There is one small snag though. You might forget that you have done this and the data mismatch error will never be seen again, even if it isn't fixed in the RTL. For safety, you should always modify the verification environment using a workaround aspect; never modify it directly. The solution to the preceding bug should be

```
<'
extend sys {
  setup() is also {

    // Turn off the error reporting for bug
    // bug0072: Data mismatch from bridge
    //
    set_check("...CHECK_BRIDGE_12...",
      WARNING);
  };
};
'>
```

Code Listing 33. workarounds.e

6.4   Reducing and deferring class complexity

Sometimes when you're writing code, say a BFM for a bus protocol, it can be hard to decide when to stop adding

functionality. Even though you've added enough functionality to do what you need to do with it today, there can be
a great temptation to add extra features just in case you might
need them in the future. Ok, your project doesn't support
protocol feature Foo, but adding it in to your BFM would
only take a couple of days, and then your code would be easily
useable on other projects. Perhaps you have come up with 10
different ways to inject errors into the protocol. You don't need
them all, of course, but for completeness, perhaps you should
just spend a week adding them in? You think they might be
useful to someone, even though they are of no use to you now.
Should you write the code anyway?

The obvious answer is no. You should just concentrate on writing the code that you need at this moment in time. You should
put some hooks in place so that the extra functionality can
be added later when it is actually needed. If this is so obvious,
why do people spend time adding the unnecessary functionality? Well, one answer is that it's fun. Let's admit it — once
you've put the effort into setting up a new piece of code, such
as a BFM, then it's nice to be able to add a decent amount of
functionality to make all of the infrastructure work (creating
files, setting up back pointers, instantiating message loggers,
etc.) worthwhile. Let's assume though that you are experienced
enough to know that this is not a great use of your time. Why
else would you put functionality in instead of just the required
hooks? If you are using OOP only, then the answer might
simply be that adding hooks is hard and not much fun.
Building in the infrastructure needed to give the end user
(which might eventually be you) enough hooks to add in the
missing functionality is tedious. It's much more enjoyable to
spend the extra time and just write the functionality now.

This could be a mistake though. To start with, the functionality you add might never be needed. If you don't need it
now, what makes you think you'll need it later? Once you

decide to add the extra functionality, then you are also committing to testing it, debugging it, documenting it, and possibly maintaining it. That's a lot of extra work that's adding nothing to your current project. But it gets worse. Even if you try to predict all the required functionality, it's almost inevitable that the end user will want to do something slightly different with your code, something that you don't support. What this means is that no matter how much time you spend now building in extra functionality, you'll probably never get it all, and you (or someone) will have to change your code later. Perhaps building the hooks in up front instead of the extra functionality would be a better, if slightly boring, use of your time.

With an AOP solution hooks are basically free. OK, you need to define an empty method in the class and call it at the right place. That's hardly taxing or time consuming. With minimal effort, you can build in the hooks required to extend the code and avoid the overhead of writing and maintaining code that might never get used.

Consider the following example scenario. You are writing a BFM for an rs232 serial transmitter (a UART). The protocol defines a variable number of data bits, an optional parity bit that can have a configurable parity, and a variable number of stop bits. For your project, you only need to support a fixed configuration, but you want to write the code in such a way that it is easily upgradeable later. The best approach here is to constantly be aware that someone may want to extend your code to add new functionality, but not to add the new functionality yourself. It isn't needed and will just delay your project.

The `transmit()` method in the BFM can be written as one large method, but that will mean that the next user will just have to replace the entire method, rewriting working code.

Instead, it is better to code `transmit()` using methods for each of the substages. For example,

```
unit uart_bfm_u{
  transmit(packet: uart_packet_s) @baud_clock is{
    transmit_startbit();
    transmit_data     ();
    transmit_parity  ();
    transmit_stopbit ();
  };
};
```

Now, new parity can be supported just by doing the following extension:

```
extend uart_bfm_u{
  transmit_parity() @baud_clock is only{
    // New functionality to transmit even/odd
    // parity
  };
};
```

This completely replaces the original code that was used to send the parity with new code that can deal with the enhanced functionality. This also has the added advantage that it is now easier to read and understand the code.

Once the new functionality has been verified and project schedules are not pressing, the old `transmit()` method can be replaced permanently by the new method by modifying the original source code directly.

6.5 Adding problem-specific functionality

Some design teams treat standard protocols as mere guidelines, happily making modifications wherever it gives them an advantage. If they are designing all of the blocks in the system, then this approach presents them with no problems — they really can do what they want. As a verification engineer, however, you will find this frustrating if you are planning to reuse some verification IP. There is something infuriatingly depressing about having some code that does almost what you want it to do, but not quite what you want it to do. It's 99% of the way there, but the remaining 1% is missing, and that might leave you with big problems.

This can have a huge schedule impact on your project. If you can't extend the existing verification IP yourself to add the functionality, then you might be faced with writing it all from scratch. Hopefully the code was written with enough hooks in place so that you can add the functionality, which, for reasons discussed previously, is more likely with an AOP solution than with an OOP solution.

Let's take the transmitter BFM for the rs232 serial protocol again. The protocol can support 5, 6, 7, or 8 data bits and 0 or 1 parity bits. For reasons best known to your designers, they want to customize the protocol to transmit 8, 16, 32, or 64 data bits and 0, 1, 2, 3, or 4 parity bits depending on the number of data bits. These options can all be specified using the design's existing register interface to the UART. All that really needs to change are the `transmit_data()` and `transmit_parity()` methods of the BFM. There is no good reason to write a complete BFM from scratch, and asking the original authors to make the rs232 transmit BFM programmable to select between "standard" mode and "custom" mode does not make sense.

The most pragmatic approach is to patch the BFM from your project. Other people can continue to use the original BFM source without modification (perhaps referenced from a repository), and only your project is affected.

6.6 Reducing the OOP-induced overhead

A section on the productivity increase that you can get from AOP wouldn't be complete without comparing the effort required to do something with OOP instead of with AOP. One reason you will be more productive with AOP than with OOP is that, for certain tasks, AOP simply requires less language overhead. An example of this is in Chapter 4 when we looked at hook methods. OOP solutions to this problem, such as functors or inherited classes with polymorphic methods, simply require more code to implement and to use. Although the amount of extra code might be small in the context of the verification environment, it still requires time to create, and that time soon mounts up.

Just look at the following example of a hook using AOP and a hook using OOP. The OOP solution requires an extra 11 lines of code, two extra classes, a virtual function, a for-each loop, a null pointer test, a dynamic array, object instantiations, and additions to an array — all for no added advantage.

```
struct foo_c{
  // --\/- Declaring the hook -\/--
  hook() is empty;
  // --/\- Declaring the hook -/\--

  do_something() is{
    outf("Main 1\n");
    // --\/- Calling the hook -\/--
    hook();
    // --/\- Calling the hook -/\--
    outf("Main 2\n");
  };
};

// --\/- Defining a concrete hook -\/--
extend foo_c{
```

```
  hook () is also{
    outf("Hook\n");
  };
};
// --/\- Defining a concrete hook -/\--

extend sys{
  init() is also{
    var foo: foo_c;
    foo = new;

    // --\/- Initializing the hooks -\/--
    // --/\- Initializing the hooks -/\--

    foo.do_something();
  };
};
```

Code Listing 34. An example of a simple AOP hook.

```
program test();

// --\/- Declaring the hook -\/--
class hook_c;
  virtual function hook();
  endfunction: hook
endclass :hook_c
// --/\- Declaring the hook -/\--

class foo_c;
  hook_base_c hooks[$];

  function do_something();
    $display("Main 1");
    // --\/- Calling the hooks -\/--
    foreach (hooks [h]) begin

      // Check for null just in case the hook
      // class has disappeared after it was
      // added
      //
```

```
      if(hooks[h] != null) begin
        hooks[h].modify_before_announcement();
      end
    end
    // --/\- Calling the hooks -/\--
    $display("Main 2");
  endfunction: do_something
endclass: foo_c

// --\/- Defining a concrete hook -\/--
class my_hook_c extends hook_c;
  function hook();
    $display("Hook");
  endfunction: hook
endclass: my_hook_c
// --/\- Defining a concrete hook -/\--

initial begin
  foo_c     foo;
  // --\/- Initializing the hooks -\/--
  my_hook_c my_hook;
  // --/\- Initializing the hooks -/\--

  foo     = new;

  // --\/- Initializing the hooks -\/--
  my_hook  = new;
  foo.hooks.push_back(my_hook);
  // --/\- Initializing the hooks -/\--

  foo.do_something();
end
endprogram: test
```

Code Listing 35. An example of a simple OOP hook.

The following code shows how hooks can be used in a monitor. The monitor in question samples all of the design's signals into an object and, before announcing to the world that there is a new set of signals to work with, it calls a hook method to give people a chance to do something to the sampled values. In this example, I want to do two separate things to the values. I want to add an offset to an address that has been sampled, and I want to invert a signal that has just had its polarity changed in the latest design release.

```
struct monitor_s{
  // --\/- Declaring the hook -\/--
  modify_before_announcement() is empty;
  // --/\- Declaring the hook -/\--

  // In a real design, this would be a proper
  // monitor thread which would consume time
  // and sample signals.
  // It's an example though, so I'm just going
  // to keep it simple.
  //
  monitor_thread() is{
    outf("Sampling Signals\n");

    // --\/- Calling the hook -\/--
    modify_before_announcement();
    // --/\- Calling the hook -/\--

    outf("New samples available\n");

  };
};

// --\/- Defining a concrete hook -\/--
// This one will add an offset to the
// sampled address
//
extend monitor_s{
  modify_before_announcement () is also{
    outf("Adding an offset to the address\n");
  };
};
// --/\- Defining a concrete hook -/\--

// --\/- Defining a concrete hook -\/--
```

```
// This one will invert one of the sampled
// signals
//
extend monitor_s{
  modify_before_announcement () is also{
    outf("Inverting one of the signals\n");
  };
};
// --/\- Defining a concrete hook -/\--

extend sys{
  init() is also{
    var monitor: monitor_s;
    monitor = new;

    // --\/- Initializing the hooks -\/--
    // --/\- Initializing the hooks -/\--

    // Call the monitor method to "sample"
    // the signals
    //
    monitor.monitor_thread();
  };
};
```

Code Listing 36. AOP version of the multiple monitor hooks.

```
program test();

// --\/- Declaring the hook -\/--
virtual class hook_base_c;
  virtual function
    modify_before_announcement();
  endfunction: modify_before_announcement
endclass: hook_base_c
// --/\- Declaring the hook -/\--

class monitor_c;
  hook_base_c hooks[$];
```

```
  // In a real design, this would be a proper
  // monitor thread which would consume time
  // and sample signals.
  // It's an example though, so I'm just going
  // to keep it simple
  //
  task monitor_thread();
    $display("Sampling Signals");
    // --\/- Calling the hook -\/--
    foreach (hooks [h]) begin
      hooks[h].modify_before_announcement();
    end
    // --/\- Calling the hook -/\--
    $display("New samples available");
  endtask: monitor_thread
endclass: monitor_c

// --\/- Defining a concrete hook -\/--
// This one will add an offset to the
// sampled address
//
class change_address_hook_c extends
hook_base_c;
  function modify_before_announcement();
    $display("Adding an offset to the
             address");
  endfunction: modify_before_announcement
endclass: change_address_hook_c
// --/\- Defining a concrete hook -/\--

// --\/- Defining a concrete hook -\/--
// This one will invert one of the sampled
// signals
//
class invert_signal_hook_c extends hook_base_c;
  function modify_before_announcement();
    $display("Inverting one of the signals");
  endfunction: modify_before_announcement
endclass: invert_signal_hook_c
// --/\- Defining a concrete hook -/\--
```

```
initial begin
  monitor_c monitor;

  // --\/- Initializing the hooks -\/--
  change_address_hook_c change_address;
  invert_signal_hook_c  invert_signal;
  // --/\- Initializing the hooks -/\--

  monitor = new;

  // --\/- Initializing the hooks -\/--
  change_address = new;
  invert_signal  = new;

  monitor.hooks.push_back(change_address);
  monitor.hooks.push_back(invert_signal);
  // --/\- Initializing the hooks -/\--

  // Call the monitor method to "sample" the
  // signals
  //
  monitor.monitor_thread();
end
endprogram: test
```

Code Listing 37. OOP version of the multiple monitor hooks.

To me, the big difference between these implementations is not really the infrastructure required to make it work, although that is an issue because the temptation not to bother is large, but the fact that the OOP solution requires experience. It's not very intuitive unless you really understand OOP. The inexperienced programmer writing the OOP version needs to understand inheritance and virtual methods, and needs to think of using a dynamic array instead of a single class handle. An inexperienced programmer writing the AOP version just needs to call an empty method.

So, yes, you can create flexible code with OOP, but why would you want to put yourself through the pain when there's an easier way?

7

AOP in Action

Putting AOP to use is something you can start doing in small phases. You might want to start by creating an OOP style verification environment as you're used to, but to use AOP to implement lots of hooks. Users can extend these from separate files (perhaps you want a "hook" aspect?). Perhaps you have a new feature to add, such as a new transaction type (an error packet), so you could begin by making it pluggable and creating an aspect for it. You might even be sitting down to write something completely new and you want to embrace AOP fully, so you decide to identify a handful of aspects that you want to deal with and structure your code accordingly.

There are many small ways to start using AOP, but all of them would be helped by having some examples, which is the point of this chapter. In here, you'll find a number of examples that come from real projects where I've applied AOP solutions. I've aimed to keep the examples as simple as possible in order to highlight the novel AOP portions. That sometimes means trivializing large parts of the example, which might give the impression that the example is unrealistic and that I don't understand your problems because yours are much bigger. This is not the case. These examples are extracted from big code, but big code that would add nothing to your understanding of AOP. Like the other examples used throughout the book, please read the inline code comments. They contain a lot of useful information.

7.1 Creating a class with a selectable algorithm

Organization	Yes	Different algorithms can be encapsulated in their own files, even though they might all be part of the same class
Pluggable code	Yes	This example shows the strategy pattern, which is designed to make code pluggable
Flexible code	Yes	By building the strategy pattern into your code, you are creating an interface that the end user can use to customize the code's operation
Productivity	Yes	The AOP solution takes less effort to implement and use than the OOP solution

This example shows how to use when-inheritance to create run-time pluggable code. There is a well-defined OOP solution that allows pluggable code called the *strategy pattern* [25]. This calls the pluggable code "strategies" and they are normally described as some form of data processing algorithm. The idea is that you have a class that needs to process some data, but the actual algorithm required to do this it is pluggable. In truth, these strategies can do anything an object can do; there is no need to limit them to data processing. The strategy pattern works by having the strategies in concrete classes that are derived from a common base class. The class that needs to use a strategy (known as the *context class*) has a handle to the strategy base class, and at runtime, this is set to an instance of the appropriate strategy. The strategy instance has to be created by the user, probably by using a factory.

This approach works with *e* as well because it supports like-inheritance. In this section though, I'm going to discuss a slightly simpler way to do it using when-inheritance and AOP. This approach has the advantage that you don't need to instantiate the correct strategy class and pass it into the object that is to use it. Because the strategy is a when-extension of a class, no new object has to be instantiated to use a strategy, allowing you to dispense with the factory and a bunch of extra class types. The AOP approach can be simplified even further at the expense of reusability. The strategies can be built into the context class itself, although this then stops you reusing them in other classes. It is fairly simple to refactor the strategy part back out into a separate class to make it generic, but unless I knew that I really did need to reuse the strategy pattern, I'd be tempted to keep it simple and just make the changes later if required.

In this example I'll show the simplest approach using AOP. If you want to make it more reusable, just add the strategies to a class used by the context class (via a handle to the strategy base class) rather than extending the context class directly. In the AOP strategy pattern, a single determinant in the context class dictates which strategy is active, and this can be changed at runtime to make a new strategy active. Because when-inheritance is used, each strategy can be defined in its own aspect, and new strategies can be easily added later.

In order to switch between strategies transparently they must all share the same interface. This interface should be defined as one or more methods in the base context class. Declare these as is undefined to ensure that you get an error if a strategy does not implement one of the interface methods.

The following code shows a template for the AOP strategy pattern. The names of the enumerated type, the context class, the strategy field, and the interface method should all be changed to something more meaningful for your application.

```
<'
// This type contains the names of the strategies the
// context class supports
//
type strategy_names_t: [];
```

```
// This is the context class. It has no default
// strategies — these have to be added later.
//
unit context_u{

  // This is the determinant that will be used to select
  // the strategy that is active.
  //
  strategy: strategy_names_t;

  // You can declare some fields and methods here that
  // can be used by all strategies

  // This is a hook called when the strategy is changed.
  // You cannot use constraints to initialize a
  // strategy, because the context unit is not generated
  // when the determinant changes. We have to initialize
  // things the old-fashioned way.
  //
  setup_strategy() is empty;

  // This is called to change the active strategy
  //
  set_strategy(s: strategy_names_t) is{
    strategy = s;
    outf("Changing strategy to %s\n", strategy);
    setup_strategy();
  };

  // This is the entry point to the strategy. The exact
  // name and prototype will depend on the strategies
  // you are encapsulating.
  //
  do_something() is undefined;
};
'>
```

Code Listing 38. A template for an AOP strategy pattern.

```
<'
// -----\/----- The STRATEGY_1 Aspect----\/-----
// Define the name of the strategy.
//
extend strategy_names_t: [STRATEGY_1];

// Extend the context class to have the STRATEGY_1.
// strategy.
//
extend STRATEGY_1 context_u{

  // --\/-- Declare some strategy-specific data --\/--

  // --/\-- Declare some strategy-specific data --/\--

  // -\/- Declare some strategy-specific methods -\/-

  // -/\- Declare some strategy-specific methods -/\-

  // This is called when the algorithm is changed to
  // STRATEGY_1
  //
  setup_strategy() is also{

    // Initialize any local fields that this strategy
    // has. Constraints will not work because the unit
    // has already been generated, and it is not
    // regenerated just because the determinant changed.
  };

  // Define the STRATEGY_1 strategy
  //
  do_something(): is also{
    // Your strategy-specific code goes here
  };
};
// -----/\----- The STRATEGY_1 Aspect -----/\-----
'>
```

Code Listing 39. A strategy template for an AOP strategy pattern.

```
<'
extend sys{
  context: context_u is instance;

  run() is also{
    // Select the strategy you want to be active...
    //
    context.set_strategy(STRATEGY_1);

    // ...and use it for something
    //
    context.do_something();

    // Now select a new strategy...
    //
    context.set_strategy(STRATEGY_2);

    // ... and do something again. It will behave
    // differently this time because a new strategy is
    // operating
    //
    context.do_something();
  };
};
'>
```

Code Listing 40. Using the AOP strategy pattern.

The following code shows an example strategy pattern in action. It is an arbiter with two arbitration schemes — round robin and slot based. The following code can be used by the arbiter to select the appropriate algorithm.

```
// Use the Round Robin algorithm
//
set_arbitration_strategy(ROUND_ROBIN);
```

```
// Use the slot-based algorithm
//
set_arbitration_strategy(SLOT_BASED);

// Use a random algorithm. This is particularly useful
// when only one algorithm is compiled into the
// verification environment, because the verification
// environment will use it without having to know which
// one it's using
//
var algorithm: arb_strategy_t;
gen algorithm;
set_arbitration_strategy(algorithm);
```

Code Listing 41. Some examples of how the available strategies plugged into a verification environment can be selected.

```
<'
// This type contains the names of the arbitration
// strategies
//
type arb_strategy_t: [];

// This is the context class—the arbiter. It has no
// default arbitration scheme—these have to be added
// later.
//
unit arbiter_u{
  // This is the determinant that will be used to select
  // the arbitration scheme is force.
  //
  arbitration_strategy: arb_strategy_t;

  // An arbiter global field that lets all the
  // arbitration strategies know how many masters there
  // are.
  //
```

```
number_of_masters: uint;
keep soft number_of_masters == 3;

// This is an arbiter global field that the arbitration
// strategies use to track the current master.
//
current_master: uint;
keep current_master == 0;


// This is a hook called when the arbitration strategy
// is changed. You cannot use constraints to
// initialize a strategy, because the unit is not
// generated when the determinant changes. We have to
// initialize things the old-fashioned way.
//
setup_strategy() is empty;


// Called to change the arbitration strategy in use.
//
set_arbitration_strategy(s: arb_strategy_t) is{
  arbitration_strategy = s;
  outf("Changing arbitration strategy to %s\n", s);
  setup_strategy();
};


// This is the entry point to the arbitration
// strategy. It is called by the arbiter to work out
// who should be granted next.
//
get_next_master_id(requesting_masters: list of uint)
                                   :uint is undefined;
};
'>
```

Code Listing 42. The arbiter context class.

```
<'
// ---\/--- The Round Robin Strategy Aspect ---\/---
// Define the name of the strategy.
//
extend arb_strategy_t: [ROUND_ROBIN];


// Extend the arbiter to have the Round Robin strategy.
//
extend ROUND_ROBIN arbiter_u{


  // Define the Round Robin strategy.
  //
  get_next_master_id(requesting_masters: list of uint):
                                        uint is also{
    // This is where the code that calculates
    // current_master will go.
  };
};
// ---/\--- The Round Robin Strategy Aspect ---/\---
'>
```

Code Listing 43. The round robin strategy aspect.

```
<'
// ----\/--- The Slot-Based Strategy Aspect ---\/---

// Define the name of the strategy.
//
extend arb_strategy_t: [SLOT_BASED];
// Extend the arbiter to have the slot-based strategy.
//
extend SLOT_BASED arbiter_u{
```

```
// --\/-- Declare some strategy-specific data --\/--
// This list contains the slot order that will be used
// to select the next master.
//
!slots         : list of uint;

!current_slot: uint;
// --/\-- Declare some strategy-specific data --/\--

// This is called when the strategy is changed to
// SLOT_BASED
//
setup() is also{
  current_slot = 0;
};

set_slots(s: list of uint) is{
  slots = s;
};

// Define the Slot based strategy.
//
get_next_master_id(requesting_masters: list of uint):
                                        uint is also{
  // This is where the code that calculates
  // current_master will go.
};
};
// ---/\--- The Slot-Based Strategy Aspect ---/\---
'>
```

Code Listing 44. The slot-based strategy aspect.

7.2   Creating a configuration interface for an eVC

Organization	Yes	Lets you keep the configuration interface separate from the core of the code
Pluggable code	Yes	Configurable features can be added or removed without editing the configuration object
Productivity	Yes	It's far easier to code a pluggable version in AOP than it is in OOP

The configuration interface to an eVC is something that's worth applying AOP to because of the number of different classes and concerns that interact with it. Configuration interfaces have the following features that make AOP an attractive solution:

1. Configuration interfaces can grow very large, so having them all in one file can be awkward. Their size can slow down editors that do on-the-fly formatting, and they can simply become difficult to navigate. It's easy to get lost inside a large file. However, you do want to be able to encapsulate your configuration interface so that users can find them and interact with them.

2. Configuration interfaces deal with many different components and features of your verification environment, and it is likely that some of these will be pluggable. Therefore, you really need to design those parts of the configuration interface to be pluggable too.

3. Configuration interfaces don't always fit into a single class. Some parts of your verification environment will already have configuration interfaces, and although you might be able to wrap these in a new class, it might be easier to just wrap them in an aspect, which will avoid a layer of indirection.

This example will show

- what aspect to use;

- how to make configuration interfaces that are pluggable;

- how to encapsulate a subcomponent's configuration interface in your eVC's configuration interface.

Deciding what aspect to use for a configuration interface is really easy. The configuration aspect is called "config" (or "configuration" if you are a fan of large file names). For instance, `config-ahb-scoreboard.e` would contain the AHB scoreboard configuration options and `config-dma.e` would contain the configuration options for the DMA. Isolating the configuration files can be done simply using `ls | grep config` or `ls config*`. The former is more suited to when you want to isolate where the configuration aspect crosses particular concerns, for example, `ls | grep config | grep ahb | grep scoreboard`. All the listed files are contributors to the AHB, scoreboard, and configuration aspect.

So now you know what to call your aspect, how do you make it pluggable, which was the second thing I was going to show you? Remember that pluggable code is simply code that can be nonintrusively added to, or removed from, your verification environment. For configuration interfaces, this is really easy to do.

It helps to think about your configuration class as a collection of layers, where each layer is a particular concern that you are configuring. As long as you ensure that the layers don't interact with each other (and there's no real reason why they should), then all you need to do is map each layer to a separate file. These layers can be excluded or included in the verification environment by simple inclusion or exclusion of the file in the manifest file.

Figure 7.1 shows a sample configuration interface class for an eVC that is used to verify an SoC. You can see that there are a large number of configuration options. Probably the most common approach to coding this would be to convert the diagram directly to code. You'd create a configuration class and put it in a single file, and just start populating it with the appropriate methods and functionality. If a new concern that had to be configured was added to the verification environment, you'd just open up the file and add the new functionality.

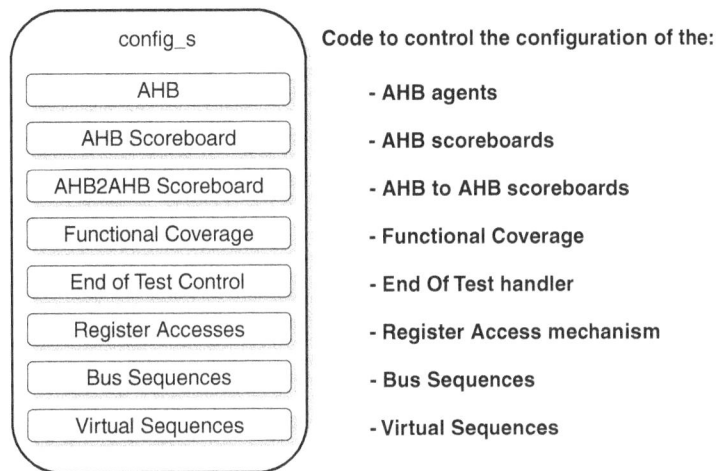

Figure 7.1   A eVC configuration interface as a class.

If you wanted to make it pluggable, and you didn't have AOP, then you'd have to start getting involved in advanced OOP techniques. You'd have to create a common abstract base class for configuration options, create concrete versions for each concern, create a configuration class that had a dynamic list of these base classes, build a mechanism to let the user find and access the one they wanted, get the user to cast the base class back to the correct concrete class so that they could access it, and build the objects at runtime before you could use the overall configuration object. It wouldn't be pretty to code or to use. I think it's fair to say most people wouldn't bother because of the added complexity.

With AOP you can get the pluggable behavior without any of this effort. Look at Figure 7.1 again. It only takes a moment to see the potential for using aspects and making each concern pluggable. In fact, you can even see the appropriate file names — config-ahb.e, config-ahb-scoreboard.e, config-functional coverage.e, config-registers.e, etc. You can read it from the picture (Figure 7.2).

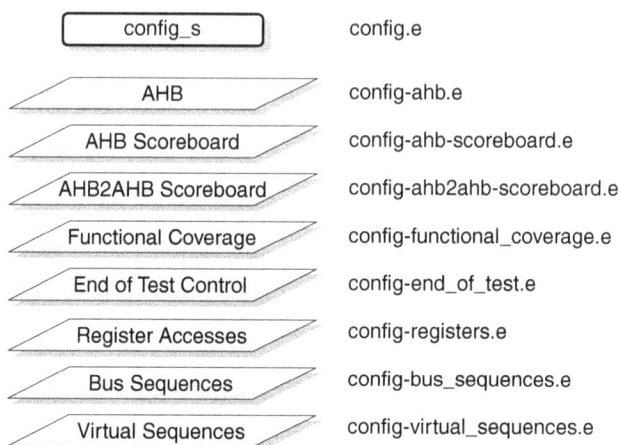

config_s	config.e
AHB	config-ahb.e
AHB Scoreboard	config-ahb-scoreboard.e
AHB2AHB Scoreboard	config-ahb2ahb-scoreboard.e
Functional Coverage	config-functional_coverage.e
End of Test Control	config-end_of_test.e
Register Accesses	config-registers.e
Bus Sequences	config-bus_sequences.e
Virtual Sequences	config-virtual_sequences.e

Figure 7.2   A eVC configuration interface as aspects.

The following code fragments show what some of this looks like as code.

```
// The eVC's runtime configuration struct. This is a
// singleton (instantiated only once) struct that is
// extended to contain the various configuration commands
// needed by various components.
//
struct config_s{
  log_change(field: string, value: string) is{
    outf("Configuration change -> %s = %s\n", field,
                                               value);
  };
};
```

Code Listing 45. The basic eVC configuration class.

```
extend config_s {

  // This field controls the end of test drain time
  //
  private drain_time: time;
  keep soft drain_time == 1000 ns;


  // The user calls this to set the drain time
  //
  set_drain_time(t: time) is{
    drain_time = t;
    log_change("drain_time", t.as_a(string));
  };


  // The end of test handler calls this to find out how
  // long to let the DUT drain before ending the test
  //
  what_is_the_drain_time(): time is {
    result = drain_time;
  };
};
```

Code Listing 46. config-end_of_test.e — the aspect for the end of test configuration.

When the user looks at this in the simulation, however, or when they access it from their code, it just looks like a normal class. Figure 7.3 shows why. The section on the left shows the empty class declaration and the individual aspects (which will be individual files as described previously). The section on the right shows the code that appears in the compiled verification environment. The weaver combines the aspects into the class that you would probably have written yourself if you didn't have AOP.

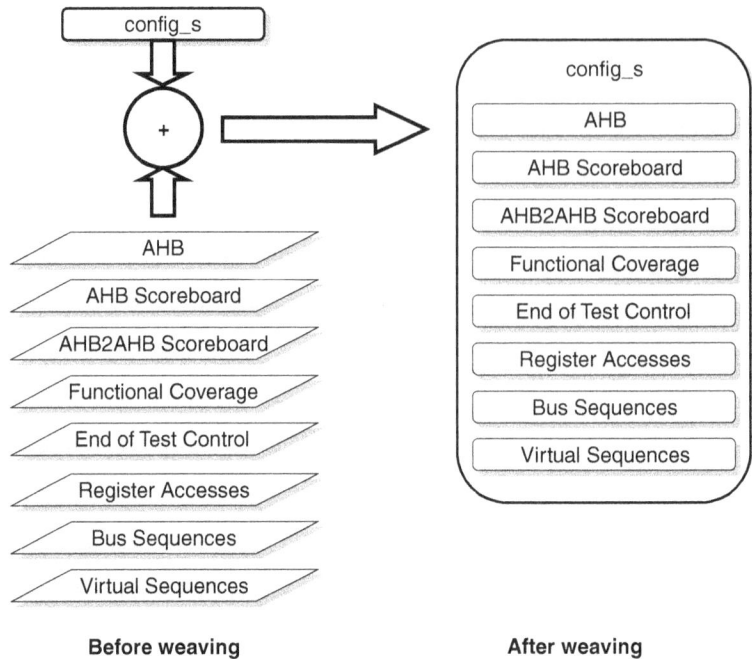

Figure 7.3   A eVC configuration interface class with aspects.

The final point I wanted to show was how to encapsulate a subcomponent's configuration interface in your eVC's configuration interface. Take a look back at the previous example, and let's pick on the AHB configuration. If your verification environment has AHB in it, then it probably uses some form of AHB eVC to drive and check the protocol. It could be an in-house solution or a commercial one, but the point is that you have incorporated a chunk of existing code into your eVC. This chunk of code probably comes with its own configuration interface.

It would be nice to be able to encapsulate that interface as part of your own eVC's interface. One way to do so is to use design patterns (the Proxy, Facade and Adaptor can all be used)[24] to incorporate the existing interface in your own interface. A simpler way is to recognize that as soon as you include something in an aspect, then it has become encapsulated. This means that you can add the existing interface to your configuration interface just by putting the appropriate configuration code in a file with config in the title. No, it's not encapsulation in terms of classes. The existing interface hasn't become part of the `config_s` class we created in the example. However, because the concerns that the configuration aspect cuts across tend to be independent from each other, there's no real need for them to appear in the same class. The encapsulation is really only useful to help people understand the code — to understand that this piece of code is part of the configuration interface. The following code shows the easy way to encapsulate an existing interface with yours. When the user searches for files to do with configuration (**ls | grep config | grep ahb**), then this one will appear, and the user will know that they can use it to configure the AHB.

```
// See "How do I limit the scope of my extensions?" on
// page 53 to see where SoC2005 comes from and why you
// need it
//
extend SoC2005 our_ahb_monitor_u {
  keep soft has_coverage                == FALSE;
  keep soft has_checks                  == TRUE;
  keep soft transaction_history_depth == 5;
};
```

Code Listing 47. config-ahb.e — the aspect for the AHB configuration.

---

[24] A good book on design patterns will tell you (a) what these are, (b) how they are different from each other, and (c) which one you should use.

7.3. Using aspects to create a layered verification environment

Organization	Yes	Code can be encapsulated across the entire verification environment based on levels of abstraction, protocol layers, functionality, or however you decide you want to organize it
Pluggable code	Yes	By partitioning code into layers, it becomes easyto replace or remove particular layers

It is common to conceptually organize a verification environment into layers, where each layer represents a particular level of abstraction or a particular functionality. This can be done fairly easily in OOP, but can AOP make it any easier?

Well, before I discuss that (and for the impatient the answer is "yes"), it's probably a good idea to discuss verification environment layering in general. After all, if you don't know what it is, or if you don't see the point, then neither the AOP nor the OOP solution will matter much to you.

Layering is just a way of organizing your verification environment. When you layer a verification environment, you're basically saying that you want to deal with it not as a collection of objects and classes, but as slices (layers) of common code that span one or more classes. You are saying that you want to deal with a verification environment's crosscutting concerns. What do I mean by "deal with"?: just that you want to perform some action, such as write, review, replace, or reuse some code. Dealing with a layer just means that you want to do something to that layer. The actual meaning of something doesn't really matter.

By layering your verification environment, you are essentially just creating a view of your code that lets you deal with it in way that doesn't care about the classes you have. For instance, instead of dealing with the BFM or the monitor, you can deal with transactions or functional coverage, not caring which classes they cut across. Doing this brings a number of benefits, such as those given here:

■ Layers allow test writers to interact with the DUT at the most appropriate level of abstraction. For example, some tests might need to drive signals directly (using the signal layer) whereas some might need to access its registers (using the register layer). Other tests might need to interact with the DUT by issuing very high-level commands (using the transaction layer). Note that these layer names are just examples. You can create any kind of layers that you think are useful.

■ Layers that are not needed during certain tests, such as high-level sequences during system testing, can be easily removed or disabled.

■ Layers allow you to replace the code in certain layers with different implementations. For example, the signal connection layer could be removed and the low-level task layer replaced with one that communicates with a SystemC model rather than an RTL model.

So, layers are just crosscutting concerns and are just slices across your code. Each layer defines a bound of responsibility, which means that the layer should only deal with certain things, and only code that deals with those things should be in the layer. This gives your verification environment a structure that can make it easier to work with.

There are a number of layer models you could apply to your verification environment. I've shown three in Table 7.1 but this isn't exhaustive — you can use any layering structure that you think makes sense for your verification environment.

In this table, the columns are layer models and the rows are layers. There's no deliberate correlation between layers that

Table 7.1   Three example layer models you could apply to your verification environment

Abstraction model	Functionality model	Domain model
Scenario layer	Test layer	Application layer
Transaction layer	Test API layer	Transaction layer
Task layer	Checks layer	Link layer
Bit layer	Coverage layer	Physical layer
	Physical configuration layer	

appear in the same row. While the "physical" and "bit" layers might contain roughly the same code if applied to a verification environment, the "coverage" layer would contain radically different code.

The abstraction model defines the layers by the abstraction level of the data that the layer operates on. For instance, the transaction layer deals with transactions and the bit layer deals with individual bits. This allows the test writers to interact with the DUT at a level where the data abstraction makes the most sense for their particular tests.

However, this is not the only view you may want to take of the verification environment. If you are only writing high-level tests, and are quite happy running in a simulator (so you don't need to swap the signal connections from RTL to an accelerator), then the abstraction model might be of little use. Instead, you may wish to view the verification environment using a different model, such as the preceding functionality model. Here, the verification environment is split into a series of layers that define what it is functionally doing, not the abstraction level it is doing it at. You may also want to view the verification environment in the layer model defined by the DUT's application domain.

I said earlier that this can be done using OOP or AOP, but that it was easier to do in AOP. I'll show an example later in OOP and in AOP to show why, but a few minutes of thought should make it pretty obvious why AOP is better at doing this.

Think back to the problem. You want to deal with your verification environment in terms of crosscutting concerns. AOP is better at doing this, because that's what it was designed to do. AOP naturally deals with crosscutting concerns (layers and aspects), whereas OOP naturally deals with dominant concerns (objects and classes). Layering requires you to make OOP do something it doesn't naturally do. This is always harder.

An example would probably help around here, and I'll start by discussing the OOP solution, because that's probably what you're more familiar with. Let's say that you have a verification environment (we'll focus on the BFM and monitor for simplicity) and you want to organize it into three layers — transaction, task, and connection. The transaction layer deals with the transactions themselves and the code that processes them, the task layer deals with the tasks that interact with the DUT (such as `read()`, `write()`, `reset()`, `configure()` etc.), and the connection layer just deals with the signal connections. To make the following discussion slightly more easy, I'll refer to the BFM and monitor classes as "vertical classes" because they look vertical when you draw them — they cover lots of different layers of functionality but in a narrow area. Initially, these vertical classes contain everything needed to make a BFM or a monitor.

Layering this verification environment in OOP requires each vertical class to be split into subclasses, each of which represent the class' contribution to different layers of the verification environment (Figure 7.4). Each of these layer classes contains the code required to implement the operation of the vertical class at the appropriate level of abstraction. These layer classes could then be linked by composition.

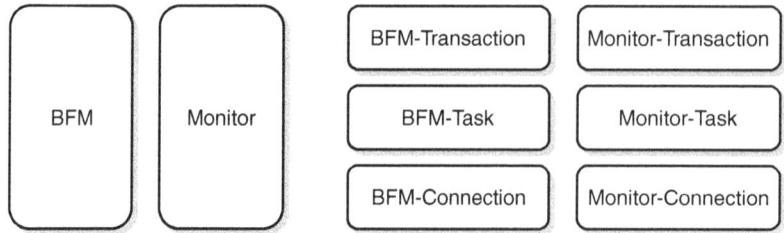

Figure 7.4   The vertical classes are shown on the left and their decomposition into horizontal layer classes is shown on the right.

The preceding solution is not really sufficient, however, if you want to be able to swap the code for a particular layer with new code. In an OOP language you need to use inheritance to create common base types. You'll have to create an abstract base class for each layer and define the layer's interface. Rather than a layer having a reference (handle or pointer) to the layer below it, it has a reference to the base class of the layer below it. The actual code that implements a layer is in a concrete class (Figure 7.5). This is a class derived from the base class.

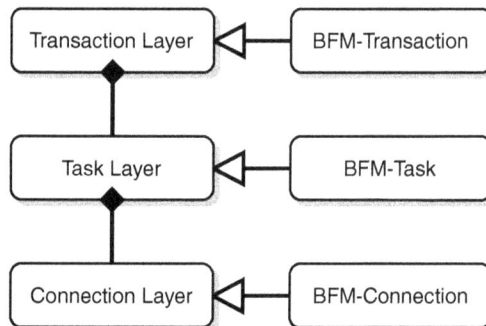

Figure 7.5   Using base classes to create verification environment layers (OOP).

A new implementation of a layer can then be swapped in transparently by setting the layer reference (the base class reference) to the new concrete layer implementation. Figure 7.6 shows an example of this. The connection layer has three concrete versions. One of these will be used when the DUT is RTL running in a simulator, the second will be used when the DUT is modeled in SystemC, and the third will be used when a hardware accelerator is used. In addition to all of this, some form of factory class will be required to instantiate the concrete layers (see "The factory pattern" on page 132 for a definition of a factory).

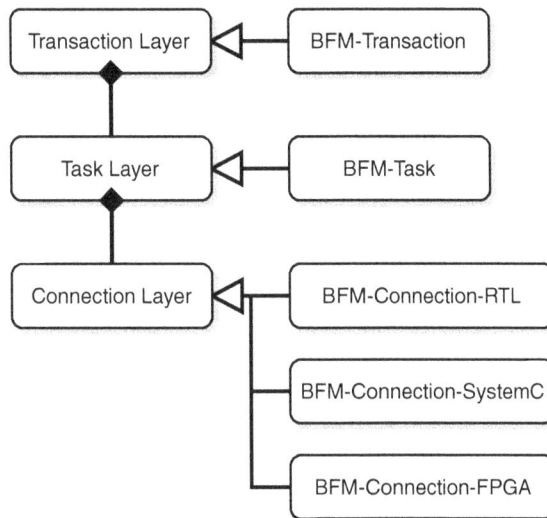

Figure 7.6   Defining concrete implementations of layers (OOP).

Implementing layering in OOP requires some infrastructure code — an abstract base class for each layer to provide a common type, individual concrete classes for each layer, base class pointers to connect the layers together, and some set-up code to create the layers and link them so that they can communicate with each other. If you're new to OOP, then the preceding description might sound a bit daunting. If you've done this before, you might just sigh and resign yourself to a bit of coding that doesn't add any verification value.

Contrast this with the AOP solution shown in Figure 7.7. Here, the vertical class is created to give structure to the design (you need to attach your aspects to something), and class extensions are used to implement the layers. The selection of a concrete layer can be done by using when-inheritance. The source code for this example follows.

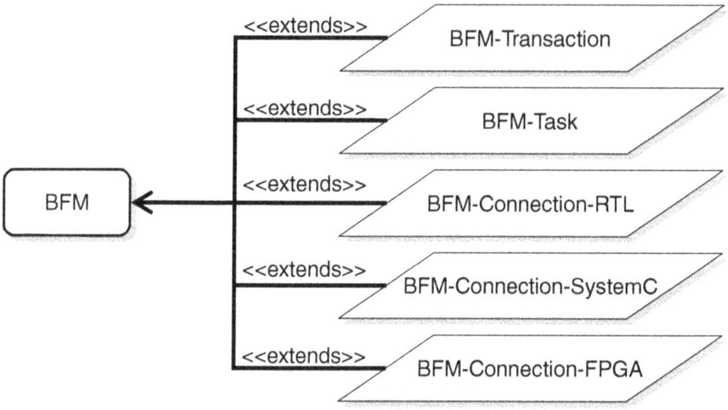

Figure 7.7   Using aspects to create verification environment layers (AOP).

```
<'
// This type will tell us how the layer is to be
// implemented - things like RTL simulation, hardware
// accelerator, etc
//
type implementation_t : [];

unit bfm_u {
  implementation : implementation_t;
  // [Code removed for clarity]

  run() is also {
    start drive_transactions();
  };

  // A hook to be extended by the actual layer code
  //
  pass_to_dut(tran: alu_transaction_s)
                        @monitor.clk is undefined;
```

```
  drive_transactions() @monitor.clk is {
    var tran: alu_transaction_s;
    while TRUE {
      tran = driver.try_next_item();


      if (tran != NULL) {
        pass_to_dut(tran);


        // Inform sequence generator, that the last item
        // was accepted:
        //
        emit driver.item_done;
      };
      wait cycle;
    };
  };
};
'>
```

Code Listing 48. The core BFM (bfm.e).

```
<'
extend implementation_t: [RTL];
extend RTL bfm_u {

  // Drive a transaction into the RTL DUT
  //
  pass_to_dut(tran: alu_transaction_s)@monitor.clk is {
    p_agent.p_a$  = tran.a;
    p_agent.p_b$  = tran.b;
    p_agent.p_op$ = tran.op.as_a(uint(bits: 3));
  };
};
'>
```

Code Listing 49. The RTL layer (bfm_connect_layer_rtl.e).

```
<'
extend implementation_t: [ACCELERATOR];
extend ACCELERATOR bfm_u {
  keep hdl_path() == "bfm";
  verilog task 'drive_transaction'(a:8, b:8, op:3);

  // Drive a transaction into the DUT on a hardware
  // accelerator. This actually drives some Verilog in
  // the simulator, which is set up to communicate with
  // the accelerator
  //
  pass_to_dut(tran: alu_transaction_s) @monitor.clk is{
    'drive_transaction'(tran.a, tran.b, tran.op);
  };
};
'>
```

Code Listing 50. The accelerator layer (bfm-connect_layer-accelerator.e).

7.4 Creating reusable layered sequences

Organization	Yes	Sequences that serve a similar purpose, but that differ by protocol, can be encapsulated in an aspect that describes the purpose, for example, ahb-stress-sequence.e and axi-stress-sequence.e
Pluggable code	Yes	The sequences are pluggable
Flexible code	Yes	New sequences can be added and existing ones can be replaced, allowing the end user to define the exact operation of the verification environment

In many verification environments, a big contribution from the verification team is in the high-level sequences. These are the sequences that implement particular use cases or nudge the design into particular operating areas where you think there might be bugs. Because they are operating at a high level, they can potentially be reused on other designs that share common characteristics. For example, I once reused a sequence that tested an SoC's bus infrastructure on five different designs. These sequences can be valuable verification IP, especially if you do lots of derivative designs.

However, it's all too easy to lock these high-level sequences to a particular design just by directly including a low-level sequence. Once you do this, your high-level sequence can only work on a design that supports that low-level sequence.[25] Let me give an example. Say you have a high-level sequence that injects some register values into your design through its debugger port. The high-level sequence is responsible for composing the correct data and sending it through the debugger port into the design. To do this, it includes a low-level sequence to drive the debugger port. Assuming that this port is a USB, the easy approach is to include a USB sequence in your high-level sequence.

That's great, until someone changes the debugger port to another protocol, say to rs232. Now this could happen due to a specification change, or because you are creating a derivative design, or because you have a completely different design and you want to reuse the knowledge already captured in the high-level sequence. The problem is that you can't use it because you hardwired a USB sequence into it.

So the problem is, how can we write high level sequences that use low-level sequences, when you don't know in advance what the low level sequences will be? How do we make the low-level sequences pluggable?

This problem is exactly the kind of problem that factories are designed to solve. You have some code that needs

---

[25] The associated infrastructure problems, such as specifying the sources and destinations in your high-level sequences so that they match the testbench they are operating in, are something I will leave to your imagination. You might want to check out the following paper for some ideas: "Shorten and Simplify SoC Verification using a Generic eVC" from www.verilab.com

to make use of some classes (sequences in this case), but it doesn't know what type those classes will be. It is essential that the high-level sequences do not contain any references to low-level, design-specific sequences. To do so would add unwanted and problematic rigidity to the verification environment. Your high-level sequence knows that it has to interact with some low-level, device-specific sequences, but it doesn't know which ones. In fact, it doesn't want to know which ones, because that would mean you had to include the eVCs for all possible protocols in your verification environment just so you could compile your high-level sequence.

The following code template shows a suitable socket that can be included in the high-level sequences. All that the high-level sequence will see is the factory and a sequence of type `any_sequence`.

```
!seq: any_sequence; // The socket

// Some missing code that works out some parameters for
// the sequence, such as the source, the destination,
// the addresses, the data and some other domain-
// specific information, and adds these to a struct
// called parameter_struct, which is used by the
// factory to initialize the low-level sequence. One
// field in parameter_struct will need to identify a
// low-level sequence. The source name or the
// destination name could be enough
//

do seq keeping{ // The plug selector
  it == sequence_factory(parameter_struct);
};
```

Code Listing 51. A basic socket template that can be used in a high-level sequence to make low-level sequences pluggable.

The following example is of a high-level sequence used to send debugger information into a design via the debugger port. In order to make the sequence reusable across different designs, the sequence makes no assumption about the type of debugger port it is to use. It could be a UART, a USB, a custom parallel protocol, etc.

- Code Listing 52 defines the factory used to generate the low-level sequences. It also defines the parameter struct that is used to pass the data into the factory, making it easily extendable in future.

- Code Listing 53 shows the high-level sequence that is used to generically send debugger information into the design.

- Code Listing 54 shows how the low-level sequence for the rs232 (UART) protocol is generated. It has been simplified for this example and leaves the issue of obtaining the sequence driver unresolved.

- Code Listing 55 shows how the high-level sequence can be used. All that is required to select the correct low-level protocol is to pass the protocol name. Everything else is handled generically.

```
<'
// This type holds the names of the protocols that can
// be used to transfer the debug information.
//
type protocols_t: [];

// This struct contains the parameters that are passed
// to the factory. It will use these to create and
// initialize the correct kind of low-level sequence
//
struct sequence_parameters_s{
  // The protocol of the sequence to generate.
  //
```

```
   !protocol : protocols_t;


   // The debugger data to inject into the design
   //
   !data     : list of uint;
};


struct sequence_factory_s{

   // The hook is extended by the various protocols.
   //
   hook(params : sequence_parameters_s,
        handled: *bool) : any_sequence is empty;

   // Call this method to get the low-level sequence
   //
   get(params :sequence_parameters_s): any_sequence is{
     var handled: bool = FALSE;
     result = hook(params, handled);

     if(handled == FALSE){
       error("\n",
         ".---(sequence_factory_s::get() error)--\n",
         "| No one claimed to know about the ",
          params.protocol, " protocol\n",
         "| I cannot continue until this is fixed\n",
         "`----------------------------------\n");
     };
   };
};
```

Code Listing 52. The factory used to generate the correct low-level
sequences for the design debug high-level sequence.

```
//              --- The virtual sequence ---
// virtual_sequence and virtual_sequence_kind are defined
// when you use the following statement:
//       sequence virtual_sequence;
// This is done elsewhere.

//            --- The high-level sequence ---
// This sequence sends some information into the design
// through the debugger port. However, we don't know
// what type of protocol will be used on this chip, so
// we have to keep this generic. The low-level sequences
// will be plugged in later.
//
extend virtual_sequence_kind: [USE_DEBUGGER];

extend USE_DEBUGGER virtual_sequence {

  // This is the sequence that will get run. A factory
  // is used to create the correct type of sequence.
  //
  !seq: any_sequence;

  // Whoever calls this sequence has to tell it which
  // protocol to use to send the debugger information.
  //
  protocol: protocols_t;

  // The raw debug data to transmit
  //
  data  : list of uint;

  body() @driver.clock is {
    // In a real device, we would probably have to
    // format the data, or do something special to enter
    // debug mode. However, to keep this example simple,
    // I won't do anything special.
    //
    var factory: sequence_factory_s    = new;
    var params : sequence_parameters_s = new;

    params.protocol = protocol;
```

```
    params.data    = data;

    do seq keeping{
      it == factory.get(params);
    };
  };
};
' >
```

Code Listing 53. The high-level sequence for injecting debugger information.

```
<'
extend protocols_t: [RS232];

extend sequence_factory_s{

  // The hook is extended by the various protocols.
  //
  hook(params : sequence_parameters_s,
       handled: *bool) : any_sequence is also{

    if(handled == FALSE and params.protocol RS232){

      // Create the basic sequence that will get
      // executed...
      //
      var seq: SIMPLE rs232_seq;
      var i   :        rs232_item_s = new;

      // ... and set it up for debugger port. Actually,
      // we are setting it up for the debugger port
      // driver which is in the verification environment,
      // hence the transmit
      //
```

```
      gen i keeping{
        .mode               == TRANSMIT;
        .use_parity         == TRUE;
        .even_parity        == TRUE;
        .number_of_stop_bits == 1;
        .data               == params.data;
      };

      gen seq keeping {
        // NOTE: You will have to assign the driver
        // here. An API method can be used
        //       driver == get_rs232_drv();
        //
        .item == i;
      };

      result  = seq;
      handled = TRUE;
    };
  };
};
```

Code Listing 54. Generating the low-level sequence.

```
<'
extend MAIN virtual_sequence{
   !send_debug_info: USE_DEBUGGER virtual_sequence;

   body() @driver.clock is {
     do send_debug_info keeping{
        // The API, and the method
        // get_debugger_port_protocol() needs to be defined
        // as part of your verification environment
```

```
        // infrastructure. I've not included this in the
        // USE_DEBUGGER virtual sequence because that
        // would then become dependent on some verification
        // environment infrastructure, and that reduces
        // the reuse potential of the high-level sequence.
        //
        .protocol == api.get_debugger_port_protocol();
    };
  };
};
'>
```

Code Listing 55. Using the high-level sequence for injecting debugger information.

7.5   Testing your verification environment

Pluggable code	Yes	The debugging code is pluggable and can be plugged in during special regression runs
Productivity	Yes	This example makes use of the fact that hooks are free in AOP and uses them to automatically verify that the verification environment is working correctly

Designs are complex and, because of this, bug prone. Verification environments tend to be even more complex than the design that they are trying to verify, so it stands to reason that they should also be bug prone. This should make you nervous, because the verification environment is one of the few measures of design quality that we have, and is normally the major factor in deciding when the design is good to go. Checking the operation of some design feature requires many steps, culminating in an error message if the behavior is wrong. We run the regressions, the verification environment doesn't complain, and the design is done. Or is it? How did you verify your verification environment? Is it actually checking at all? How did you verify that your checks worked in the first place? How did you verify that they are still working? How do you know someone didn't add `set_check("...", IGNORE)` to the verification environment and switch off all error reporting.[26] Wouldn't it be nice if there was an easy way to test the verification environment?

There are two potential problems that will cause your verification environment to miss bugs:

- Your checks don't trigger correctly;

- Your error messages are switched off.

Catching both of these can be done by forcing the error condition to occur and checking that the appropriate error message appears. If it didn't, then one of the two conditions is true.

There are two common ways of injecting error conditions into a verification environment. One approach is to modify the RTL to inject errors. Simply force some errors into the design and check that they are detected by the verification environment. There are some downsides to this approach, the first of which is that it isn't always possible to do. Verification teams are not always given write access to the RTL, and even if they are, it can be hard to control the injection of the bugs. Some bugs are actually quite subtle and hard to deliberately inject. Besides, people get nervous and start to twitch when they find out that you are deliberately putting bugs into the design.

---

[26] This kind of stupidity sometimes turns up in eVCs that you include in your testbench. It's worth grepping for this when someone delivers code to you.

An alternative approach, and one widely advocated in software design, is to write unit tests for your code. Unit tests are like mini verification environments for a class. A known issue with this approach is that it is sometimes really difficult to instantiate a class so that you can test it [26]. Many classes simply cannot live in isolation — they get information from other classes, they probe the RTL, they instantiate other classes, etc. Even instantiating these classes so that you can test them can require significant effort, and you might end up just recreating large portions of the verification environment.

So if we can't always change the RTL and we can't always do class unit testing, what other options do we have? Well, AOP comes to our rescue here as well. Remember that every method call in an AOP verification environment is a free hook point. In fact, it's two free hook points, one just before the method is called and one just after it is called. As long as your verification environment uses methods (and it would be pretty hard to avoid them), then you can add hooks into the verification environment that can inject the required bugs. Or more correctly, they can inject the symptoms of the bug. For instance, you can verify that a scoreboard is correct by modifying the monitor that supplies it with data. If you corrupt one of the fields in the monitor's transaction and the scoreboard doesn't report an error, you know something is wrong. And it gets better. You can do it without having to write mini verification environments for your classes, you can do it without having to understand or modify the design, and you get all the features and control of a proper programming language.

The following example shows how the operation of a check can be verified. In this case, the check is for an ALU. It gets a transaction from the monitor which tells it what the inputs to the ALU were, what the operation was, and what the ALU's result was. The check simply calculates its own result and compares this with the ALU's result. The entry point to the check is the `check_operation()` method, which checks that the transaction passed as a parameter is correct. Code Listing 56 simply adds a prehook to this method to make sure that the calculation is not correct. If the checker doesn't issue an error, then it is broken.

```
<'
package alu;

extend TRUE'has_checker monitor_u {
  cur_transaction : alu_transaction_s;

  on e_transaction_complete{
    check_operation(get_finished_transaction());
  };


  // [Code removed for clarity]
  check_operation(tran: alu_transaction_s) is{

    // If the ALU operation is an ADD, check that it
    // actually added the operands. trans.res is the
    // result we received from the hardware.
    //
    case tran.op {
      ADD: {
        if tran.expecting_overflow() == NO_OVERFLOW {
          check that tran.res == tran.a + tran.b else
          dut_error("[SCOREBOARD_ERROR_01]
            The result from the ALU was incorrect");
        };
      };
```

```
        // [Code that checks the other operations removed
        // for clarity]
      };
    };
  };
```

Code Listing 56. Code for ALU scoreboard (sanitized).

```
<'
package alu;


extend TRUE'has_checker monitor_u {

  // This flag will be set to TRUE when we force error_01
  // to occur.
  //
  !forced_error_01: bool;

  // Pre-hook
  // --------
  // Hook into the method that does the check, and force
  // it to fail. To do this, we're going to fake an RTL
  // bug by modifying the reported result. Because the
  // result seen by the checker is wrong. it should
  // issue an error.
  //
  check_operation(tran: alu_transaction_s) is first{
    forced_error_01 = FALSE;
    message(LOW, "Injecting a bug into the verification
                  environment to test the scoreboard");
    tran.res -=1;
    forced_error_01 = TRUE;
  };
};
'>
```

Code Listing 57. Code to force scoreboard errors.

Testing your verification environment by injecting errors is therefore quite straight forward. By hooking into existing methods, you can inject error scenarios directly into the verification environment. No matter what the design actually does, you have the ability, at no extra development cost, to overwrite its behavior and fool the verification environment into believing that the design got it wrong. Just watch for the error message appearing or not.

This is useful when you are developing your verification environment, but it would be nice if this could be automated and added to your regression. It would be nice if your code itself could check that the error messages actually appeared when expected. You can do this by making use of *e*'s check handling mechanism. When a call to `dut_error()` occurs and the check is still switched on, then `pre_error()` in `dut_error_struct` is invoked for the check. We can add a hook to the call and set a flag to record the fact that the check actually reported an error. Another hook, added to the end of the check method itself, can then look at the flag and issue an error if it wasn't set. The flow is as follows:

1. Add a hook to the start of the check method to force the error condition to occur;

2. Extend `dut_error_struct` to look for the error message. Set a flag if the error was reported;

3. Add a hook to the end of the check method and look at the flag. We know we forced the error condition, so if the flag is still false, i.e., not set, then the error was not reported by the verification environment. If this happens, issue our own error using `error()`. Errors issued in this way cannot be switched off without directly removing the call from the verification environment.

The following code extends the previous example to make the verification of the environment automatic. At the start of your regression run you should run a simulation that loads this file.[27] If your verification environment is not reporting errors correctly, the simulation will fail.

```
<'
extend TRUE'has_checker monitor_u{

  // We will increment this field if the check fires.
  //
  error_01_fired: uint;
  keep error_01_fired == 0;

  // Post-hook
  // ---------
  // Hook into the method and check if an error was
  // triggered. If not, complain.
  //
  check_operation(tran: alu_transaction_s) is also{
    if(forced_error_01 == TRUE){
      if(error_01_fired == 0){

        // The fired count is still 0, which means that
        // the check didn't fire at all. That's bad, so
        // issue an error.
        //
        outf("--(verification environment Verification)----\n");
        error("I forced SCOREBOARD_ERROR_01 to fire and nothing
              was reported. Something is wrong with the
              verification environment\n");
    } else if(error_01_fired == 1) {
```

----

[27] Which is a perfect example of pluggable code.

```
          // The check did fire. Print a message that says
          // this, and then downgrade the check to an
          // IGNORE. We don't need to verify it again.
          // To prevent this branch getting called
          // next time, increment the fired flag again.
          //
          outf("--(Verification Environment Verification)------\n");
          outf("Successfully verified that SCOREBOARD_ERROR_01\n");
          outf("is working. "It's being downgraded to IGNORE  n");
          outf("to allow other checks to be verified.          \n");
          outf("-------------------------------------------\n");
          set_check("...SCOREBOARD_ERROR_01...", IGNORE);


          // Increment it to 2. Because the check is now
          // IGNORE, dut_error_struct will not get called
          // for this again, and it will stay at 2. There's
          // no chance of a wrap round.
          //
          error_01_fired +=1;
        };
      };
    };
  };
};
// Set up dut_error_struct to intercept the error
// message, and downgrade it to a WARNING. This lets the
// user see that it really did fire, but the simulation
// should be able to continue—we probably want to verify
// other checks.
//
// Increment the fired count for this check.
//
extend dut_error_struct{
  pre_error() is also{
    if (str_match(get_message(),
            "...SCOREBOARD_ERROR_01...")){
      if (source_struct() is a TRUE'has_checker
                                    monitor_u (s)){
        if(s.forced_error_01 == TRUE){
          s.error_01_fired +=1;
        };
```

```
                // Set the check to a warning so that the
                // verification environment can continue.
                // We have to throw away the results of this
                // verification environment because we might
                // have forced a failure when one actually
                // occurred and ignored it because of this.
                //
                set_check_effect(WARNING);
                outf("--(Verification Environment Verification)------\n");
                outf("Please ignore the following DUT_ERROR message \n");
                outf("about SCOREBOARD_ERROR_01. The verification   \n");
                outf("environment is being verified, so any reported\n");
                outf("DUT errors might be invalid.                  \n");
                outf("----------------------------------------------\n");
            };
        };
      };
    };
   '>
```

Code Listing 58. Code to automatically check that the verification environment is reporting scoreboard errors.

7.6 Debugging using AOP

Pluggable code	Yes	The code needed to debug a problem, class, or feature can be encapsulated as an aspect, plugged into the verification environment when required, and unplugged when it isn't required
Productivity	Yes	Adding the code nonintrusively allows you to set up and modify the debug code more quickly than if you had to intrusively add it to many files.

Debugging a complex verification environment that's stimulating a complex design is, well, complex. Trying to work out what's going wrong might involve logging select information across multiple threads, numerous objects, and thousands of clock cycles. It might involve forcing data into obscure places in the verification environment. It might involve replacing functionality that's just obscuring the problem. It will involve adding debug messages into the code.[28]

In short, it will involve adding special code to the verification environment. Now adding debug code directly into the verification environment can cause some problems. To start with, the debug code obscures the code you are trying to analyze. The more debug code you add, the harder it becomes to review the real program code; you can see less of it at one time. The debug code also becomes scattered throughout the code base, which can cause performance problems or even bugs if you forget to remove a small piece that's changing some internal data or behavior. You can also "lose" debug code in the verification environment. Almost everyone will have encountered those debug messages that appear in the log file but prove to be remarkably difficult to track down again in the code base.

And then comes the dilemma when you have finished with it. The obvious thing to do is just delete all of the code. After all, you've fixed the bug. However, the debug code can be complex, and perhaps you think it might be useful again. There's something slightly depressing about having to rewrite debugging code to solve a different bug that affecting an area that had already been annotated. Deleting the debug code also comes with the risk that you'll accidentally delete a line of real code at the same time.

---

[28] There are some people who frown at the use of debug messages, citing the fact that you should debug with a debugger. Well, debuggers are fun, and I do use them, but I find that they force me to work at a low level of abstraction, and once I've stepped beyond a point in time, I can't go back and analyze it again. In addition, I have to be there with a debugger. Adding messages to my code lets me go home and leave a simulation running overnight, collecting scores of high-level and customized information that I can peruse at my leisure the next day.

But leaving the code in place either requires you to write a control mechanism that lets you turn it on and off or to just comment it out. Both of these obscure the program flow, and the commented out code just creates maintenance problems.

You might already have some ideas why AOP can make life better here. If you recognize that the code needed to debug a problem, class, or feature is an aspect, then you'll recognize that not only can it be nonintrusively added to the verification environment, but that it can be encapsulated so that it doesn't obscure the real code, that it can be removed without discarding it, and that it can be reintroduced without having to write control structures for doing so.

So what can you do with AOP to debug a simulation? The answer is just about anything you need to do to work out where the bug is. AOP's extension, advice, and introductions allow you to do the following:

- Add *trace debugging* by adding `is first` and `is also` pairs to record the entry to a method, its parameters, the exit from a method, and its return value;

- *Mutate inputs* by adding `is first` advice to modify the inputs to a method to force a certain state or behavior;

- *Mutate outputs* by adding `is also` advice to modify the outputs of a method to force a certain state or behavior;

- *Modify behavior* by using `is first` and/or `is also` advice to add additional functionality to a method;

- *Replace behavior* by using `is only` advice to completely replace some functionality;

- *Add or modify constraints* to force the verification environment to operate in a specific area of the problem space;

- *Add coverage* just so you can check what's happening during a debug simulation.

What AOP cannot do, however, is let you add or change functionality at places other than at method calls. If you remember from earlier in the book, advice (in the form of functional code) can only be added to method calls, so if you need to add a debug message at a point that doesn't have a method call, then you're out of luck. You will have to go and intrusively edit the verification environment's code. However, rather than adding all of the debug messages inline, just add a hook method or refactor the code into smaller methods. Whatever way you do it, adding a method call where you need the debug messages will minimize the tangling of debug code with the verification environment and lets you regain the advantages of AOP.

The following example shows many of the preceding debug features. The BFM has a single method called `drive_item()`, which takes a `transfer_item_s` struct and returns a Boolean value. The aspect in debug-bfm.e is used to add trace debugging to this method and to mutate the inputs and outputs. Mutating the inputs and outputs is a simple form of behavior modification, so this is effectively shown as well.

```
<'
type transfer_item_status_t: [NOT_PROCESSED,
                              COMPLETE_OK,
                              COMPLETE_ERROR];
struct transfer_item_s{
  address : uint( bits:32);
  data    : uint( bits:32);

  status: transfer_item_status_t;
  keep soft status == NOT_PROCESSED;
};
'>
```

Code Listing 59. transfer_item_s from the debugging example.

```
<'
unit bfm_u{
  drive_item(tfr: transfer_item_s) : bool is {
    message(LOW, "Driving the following item:") {
      outf("Address = %#X\n", tfr.address);
      outf("Data    = %#X\n", tfr.data);
    };
    tfr.status = COMPLETE_OK;
    result     = TRUE;
  };
};
'>
```

Code Listing 60. bfm.e from the debugging example.

```
<'
extend sys{
  bfm: bfm_u is instance;

  run() is also{
    var tfr: transfer_item_s;
    gen tfr keeping{
      .address == 0;
      .data    == 0xdeadbeef;
    };
    outf("bfm::drive_item() returned %s\n",
               bfm.drive_item(tfr));
  };
};
'>
```

Code Listing 61. testbench.e from the debugging example.

```
<'
extend bfm_u{

  // Input mutation
  //
  drive_item(tfr: transfer_item_s) :bool is first {
```

```
   // Set the address to a known value to force a specific
   // error
   //
   tfr.address = 0x100;
   message(LOW, "[Input mutation] changing the address
                 passed to bfm_u:: drive_item() to:"){
     outf("Address = %#X\n", tfr.address);
   };
 };

 // Output mutation
 //
 drive_item(tfr: transfer_item_s) :bool is also {
   // By changing the status, we can force the verification
   // environment into a known bug condition.
   //
   tfr.status = COMPLETE_ERROR;
   message(LOW, "[Output mutation] changing the status
                 returned from bfm_u::drive_item() to:"){
     outf("Status = %s\n", tfr.status);
   };

   // Also change the return value to show that the method
   // failed. This mechanism can also be used to force a bug
   // into the verification environment to help verify it
   //
   result = FALSE;
 };

 // Trace debugging
 //
 drive_item(tfr: transfer_item_s) :bool is first {
   message(LOW, "[Trace debug] bfm_u:: drive_item() being
                 called with:"){
     outf("Address = %#X\n", tfr.address);
     outf("Data    = %#X\n", tfr.data);
   };
 };
```

```
drive_item(tfr: transfer_item_s) :bool is also {
    message(LOW,  "[Trace debug] bfm_u::drive_item() exited"){
        outf("Status = %s\n", tfr.status);
    };
  };
};
'>
```

Code Listing 62. debug-bfm.e from the debugging example.

7.7 Encapsulating tests

Organization	Yes	Multiple pieces of code dealing with multiple parts of the verification environment can be brought together and encapsulated in one file

I thought I'd give you an example that breaks one of my three rules about mapping aspects to files. The reason for this is to show that it's always a good idea to think about what you're doing rather than blindly applying "rules." Earlier on I said that when you map aspects to files, you should try to minimize the number of concerns in a file. It was my third rule in "A word about style," on page 69. If you try to apply this to one of the most common aspects in verification environment design, a test, then no one will thank you.

Tests are probably the most common, obvious, and wide reaching of all crosscutting concerns in a verification environment. They are so obvious that some people advise that AOP should *only* be used for tests (but I disagree). A test has many duties to perform, and it has to interact with many things to do them. It has to set up the environment that it operates in (for example, set the logging verbosities, the watchdog timeouts, the coverage that will or will not be recorded, and which checks to switch off), the physical composition of the verification environment (for example, how many peripherals will take part in the test), and individual elements in the verification environment (for example, what errors slave 3 should inject and which memory addresses should return when accessed). Once the simulation has started, the test has to control everything, giving individual instruction where necessary (for example, tell the reset generator when to issue a warm reset) and ensuring that the right stimuli is injected at the right times.

Let's assume that your DUT is a DMA and you are writing a test to check how it deals with handshaking errors and warm resets during transfers. Your test needs to do the following:

- Program the source peripheral to use software handshaking;

- Configure the destination peripheral to use hardware handshaking;

- Change the source and destination peripherals' BFMs to inject errors into the handshaking protocol;

- Change the source and destination peripherals so that they tell the reset generator when they have introduced an error;

- Modify the reset generator to generate a warm reset after a certain number of protocol errors and to generate the reset during an error;

- Repeatedly configure the DUT to do various types of transfers.

The test involves interactions with the source and destination peripherals (peripheral aspect, BFM aspect, error aspect), the

DUT's configuration interface sequences (DUT and DUT configuration aspect), and the reset generator (reset aspect). Some of these are programmatically configured and others are physically modified to give the desired behavior. In addition to these, the test probably also configures some loggers (logging aspect and the debugging aspect) and maybe even Specman itself (Specman configuration aspect).

This all means that a test is probably one of the biggest crosscutting concerns in your verification environment. Biggest in terms of the number of other concerns that it interacts with anyway. If you follow the third rule I gave earlier (on page 70), then each of your tests will suddenly become composed of many, many small files, each one representing the interaction between your test and a particular crosscutting concern. For example, if your test is to check how your DMA deals with handshaking errors and warm resets during transfers (the example given previously), then you might end up with the following files:

- `test-handshaking_errors-warm_resets-source_peripheral.e;`

- `test-handshaking_errors-warm_resets-dest_peripheral.e;`

- `test-handshaking_errors-warm_resets-reset_generator.e;`

- `test-handshaking_errors-warm_resets-configure_dut.e;`

- `test-handshaking_errors-warm_resets-logging.e.`

This is a bit ridiculous. Because tests names tend to be descriptive so that people can understand them from the file name, test file names can be quite large even before adding on the "test_" aspect identifier or the names of the other aspects contained in the file. Therefore, ignore my third rule and instead just name your test file after what it is trying to do. For example, test short random transfers.e, check receive mode.e, or warm reset.e.

Now a test file can still become very large, large enough that you might need to split it up just to improve your editor's performance, and despite of what I've just said, you might also want to deal with some crosscutting concerns separately.[29] For instance, if you wanted to handle Specman configuration separately from the core test, then check receive mode-config specman.e would contain the Specman configuration options. In a break from my normal advice, I would not have a manifest file called -top.e to load the test. Either name the manifest file as the test (check receive mode-top.e should be check receive mode.e) or do direct file imports from the main test file. The important thing here is that the entry point to the test has the descriptive name.

Also, pay close attention to your regression environment when you come to name your tests. Many environments automatically pick up tests, either by searching for specially named files or by taking all files in a certain directory. Any scheme you use to organize your test aspects must fit with your regression environment.

---

[29] See—rules are really just guidelines. Sometimes they fit and sometimes they don't.

8

Analyzing *e* Code

Who cares how it works, just as long as it gives the right answer?

Jeff Scholnik

I normally find myself asking two simple questions when I try to understand a verification environment's architecture or operation:

- "Where is *that* declared?"

- "What *exactly* is getting executed?"

It doesn't matter whether the code belongs to someone else or whether I'm simply revisiting some of my code after an absence; after a certain amount of time away from a particular area of the verification environment I forget the exact details of how it does what it does. Even if a verification environment follows the guidelines in Chapter 3, it can still be tricky to work out what aspect some functionality belongs to or what file in the aspect contains the code.[30] The size of the code isn't really a factor either, because almost all

---

[30] Note that "tricky" is still much preferable to the "impossible" you'd have with a badly structured testbench.

verification environments are big enough to keep me from holding them entirely in my head at one time.

Some people blame AOP for this. They say that advice and introductions make it impossible to understand the operation of a verification environment. Adding class members from other files, calling additional code when you call a method, or replacing a method entirely are the reasons why they can't understand an *e* verification environment. Just don't get them started on macros!

I don't buy this tale of *e* or AOP code being impossible to understand. Yes, it can be difficult, but that's really just due to the fact that I can't read, memorize, and comprehend thousands of lines of software all at the same time. I don't believe that there is anything inherent in *e* or AOP that makes them worse than any other programming language or paradigm. Big code is simply hard to understand. Every reason I've heard to explain why *e* code is hard to understand I've seen in action elsewhere. Want an example? Just try understanding the operation of a SystemC verification environment that's making full use of multiple inheritance, templates, polymorphism, and macros and you'll understand what I mean. If you're looking at a pointer to a base class and you want to know what actually gets called when you call a method, then you're going to have to do a runtime analysis of the code. Don't have a SystemC testbench to hand? Just try reading one of those monster Perl scripts written by a regular expression fetishist instead.

I think there are two reasons why *e* and AOP have bad reputations for not being understandable. The first is simply that people are not used to it. They expect to see a design organized by structure, not by function. They expect to open up a file and see a single class in its entirety. The idea that a single class is now spread across multiple files confuses people. They expect the operation of the code to be the same no matter in what order it's loaded.[31] They expect overridden methods to be called in an easy to understand order.

The second reason is tool support. Although Specman comes with a selection of tools and commands to help you analyze a verification environment, it lacks an intuitive, easy-to-use solution that lets you fully explore a design. It has no integrated development environment that will let you understand the structure of your design while you are editing it. Instead, you have to load your verification environment into Specview and use the Data Browser, the `collect` command, the Source Searcher, and the debugger to analyze your verification environment.[32] You don't always get the information you need either.

So in this chapter I'll introduce you to a script I use to do most of my *e* code analysis. Although I do still occasionally use the tools in Specman, this script gives me a quick way to find out the information I need from the command line.

8.1 The *e* toolkit

The *e* toolkit is a script that I use for analyzing *e* verification environments, and it's freely downloadable from www.verilab.com. The basic command for starting the script is `etk.pl.` This will present you with the general help. The first thing you need to do is decide what *e* files you are going to analyze. By default, the script will do a recursive search

---

[31] Although why, I don't know. Any code using preprocessor commands can subtly change form depending on the load order.

[32] You can find more information about these in the Specman Elite documentation.

for ._e_ files from the current working directory and use these files. If you want more control, then the `--file` option lets you specify a manifest file that will contain the paths to the files to analyze. You can build this quite easily from the Specman log file if you need to work out exactly what a verification environment loads and in what order. An example manifest file (filelist.txt) is as follows:

```
/home/e/examples/transaction.e
/home/e/examples/sequence.e
/home/e/examples/env_h.e
/home/e/examples/agent_h.e
/home/e/examples/monitor_h.e
/home/e/examples/monitor.e
/home/e/examples/checker.e
/home/e/examples/coverage.e
/home/e/examples/bfm.e
/home/e/examples/agent.e
/home/e/examples/env.e
/home/e/examples/end_test.e
```

So to analyze these files, the command would be

`etk.pl --files filelist.txt`

Of course, you have to give it a command to tell it what you're looking for, but I'll get to that later. There is a `--show` option that gives you five different ways to control what information is displayed. You can choose to see the following:

- ■ `files:` shows the files where the item you are looking for occurs;

- ■ `items:` shows the items found, but with no context or location information;

- **context:** shows the items found and their context. For instance, methods found will be shown with the name of the class they are found in;

- **summary:** shows a comma-separated one-line summary that contains file names, line numbers, item names, and context. This mode works especially well with spreadsheet tools that accept comma-separated value files;

- **all:** shows everything, including the lines of code.

Some of the show options only become relevant when you are searching for multiple items. For instance, the **items** option doesn't tell you anything useful when you prespecify the exact item you were looking for, except for the fact that it was found. You'll see that in this example. It becomes very useful, however, when you use wild cards to specify the items to search for.

To show how the different options affect the output, the following examples all look for the declaration and extension of the `drive_transactions` method in the `bfm_u` class. All that changes is the `--show` option:

```
etk.pl --show files method bfm_u drive_transactions
  ./e/bfm.e
```

```
etk.pl --show items method bfm_u
drive_transactions
  drive_transactions
```

```
etk.pl --show context method bfm_u
drive_transactions
  bfm_u::drive_transactions
```

```
etk.pl --show summary method bfm_u
drive_transactions
  Class, Method, Encapsulation, Kind, Start Line,
  End Line, File
```

```
bfm_u, drive_transactions, public, definition [is],
31, 48, ./e/bfm.e
```

etk.pl --show all method bfm_u
drive_transactions

```
.-------------+-------------------------------------
|             | Method       : bfm_u::drive_trans...
|             | Kind         : definition [is]
|             | Encapsulation: public
|             | File         : ./e/bfm.e
|   Lines     |              : 31 to 48
+-------------+-------------------------------------
|             |
| [ 31 - 31]  | drive_transactions()@monitor.clk is{
| [ 32 - 32]  |     var tran: alu_transaction_s;
| [ 33 - 33]  |     while TRUE {
| [ 35 - 35]  |       tran = driver.try_next_item();
| [ 39 - 39]  |       if (tran != NULL) {
| [ 40 - 40]  |           p_agent.p_a$  = tran.a;
| [ 41 - 41]  |           p_agent.p_b$  = tran.b;
| [ 42 - 42]  |           p_agent.p_op$ = tran.op;
| [ 44 - 44]  |           emit driver.item_done;
| [ 45 - 45]  |       };
| [ 46 - 46]  |     wait cycle;
| [ 47 - 47]  |     };
| [ 48 - 48]  | };
|             |
`-------------+-------------------------------------
```

Because some of the lines of code shown by the **--show all** option are wider than the page, I've truncated them in the examples with an ellipse (. . .). The real script doesn't do this.

Before I go on to the commands themselves, the last thing to explain is how the search terms work. Each command needs information from you, normally the name of the item you are looking for and the context where the program is to look.

So for instance, if you are searching for a method, you have to give the name of the method and the class name that the method belongs to. These names are used as Perl regular expressions, so you can pass in quite complex search terms. Some examples are as follows:

- `'.*_u'`: find all items ending with _u

- `'\wfm_(u|s)'`: find all items starting with an alphanumeric character (\w) followed by "fm_" followed by a "u" or an "s"

- `'.*'`: find any item.

Note that single quotes are used to surround complex expressions to prevent the shell from interpreting and removing certain characters.

8.2 Finding class declarations and extensions

PROBLEM   I need to find the declaration and/or the extensions of a class. I haven't used class names as an aspect, so how do I find this information?

SOLUTION   The *e* toolkit provides the following three commands to help you with this:

- `cd`: Short for **C**lass **D**eclaration, this command will find the definition of the named class;

- `ce`: Short for **C**lass **E**xtensions, this command will find the extensions of the named class;

- `class`: This command combines the previous two and finds the declaration and the extensions of the named class.

EXAMPLE   To find the names of all classes in the verification environ-
          ment (this is an excellent way to start exploring the structure
          of a verification environment):

```
etk.pl --show items cd '.*'
  agent_u
  alu_transaction_s
  bfm_u
  env_u
  monitor_u
```

To find all files that extend the `agent_u` class:

```
etk.pl --show files ce agent_u
  ./e/agent.e
```

To see the code for the definition and the extensions of the
`alu_transaction_s` class:

```
etk.pl --show all class alu_transaction_s
```

```
.-------------+---------------------------------------------
|             | Name          : alu_transaction_s
|             | Kind          : definition
|             | File          : ./e/transaction.e
|    Lines    |               : 17 to 69
+-------------+---------------------------------------------
|             |
| [ 17 -  17] |   struct alu_transaction_s like an...
| [ 18 -  18] |     a          : int(bits: 8);
| [ 19 -  19] |     b          : int(bits: 8);
| [ 20 -  20] |     op         : alu_op_t;
| [ 21 -  21] |     !res       : int(bits:8);
| [ 22 -  22] |     !overflow: bit;
| [ 34 -  34] |     keep value(op) == SUB => soft...
| [ 36 -  36] |       print_fields() is{
| [ 37 -  37] |         outf("\n");
| [ 38 -  38] |         outf("a = %d (0b%b)\n", a,...
| [ 39 -  39] |         outf("b = %d (0b%b)\n", b,...
```

```
|  [ 40 -   40] |      outf("op = %s\n", op.as_a(...
|  [ 41 -   41] |      outf("overflow  = %d\n", ...
|  [ 42 -   42] |      outf("result = %d (0b%b)\n...
|  [ 43 -   43] |    };
|  [ 45 -   45] |    do_print() is only{
|  [ 46 -   46] |      print_fields();
|  [ 47 -   47] |    };
|  [ 50 -   51] |    expecting_overflow(): overflo...
|  [ 52 -   52] |     var answer: int;
|  [ 54 -   54] |     result = NO_OVERFLOW;
|  [ 55 -   55] |     case op {
|  [ 56 -   56] |        ADD:{ answer = a+b;};
|  [ 57 -   57] |        SUB:{ answer = a-b;};
|  [ 58 -   58] |     };
|  [ 60 -   60] |     if (answer > 127) {
|  [ 61 -   61] |        result = TOO_POSITIVE;
|  [ 62 -   62] |     };
|  [ 63 -   63] |     if (answer < -128){
|  [ 64 -   64] |        result = TOO_NEGATIVE;
|  [ 65 -   65] |     };
|  [ 66 -   66] |    };
|  [ 69 -   69] |  };
`-------------+------------------------------------


.-------------+------------------------------------
|             | Name       : alu_transaction_s
|             | Kind       : extension
|             | File       : ./test/error_test.e
|    Lines    |            : 27 to 35
+-------------+------------------------------------
|             |
|  [ 27 -   27] | extend alu_transaction_s{
|  [ 30 -   30] |    keep b.reset_soft();
|  [ 31 -   31] |    keep soft b == select{
|  [ 32 -   32] |       2: others;
|  [ 33 -   33] |       8: min;
|  [ 34 -   34] |    };
|  [ 35 -   35] |  };
`-------------+------------------------------------
```

8.3   Finding the class inheritance hierarchy

PROBLEM   I want to see the like-inheritance hierarchy for a class.

SOLUTION   The *e* toolkit provides the **ch** command (**C**lass **H**ierarchy) to
               do this for you.

EXAMPLE   To find the hierarchy of the alu_transaction_s struct:

```
etk.pl --show context ch alu_transaction_s
   [alu_transaction_s] is derived from
   [any_sequence_item]
```

8.4   Finding the determinants used by
a class

PROBLEM   I want to see all of the fields in a class that are being used as
               determinants.

SOLUTION   The *e* toolkit provides the **cdet** command (**C**lass **De**termi-
               nants) to do this for you.

DISCUSSION   Class determinants are class properties that are used to
               create class subtypes using when-inheritance. Common
               examples are an eVC's environment name or the ACTIVE/
               PASSIVE flag found in eVC agents. This command shows
               all the properties that are used to extend a class. It does not
               show which combinations of values were used.

EXAMPLE   To find the determinant properties of the monitor_u
               struct,

```
etk.pl --show all cdet monitor_u
   Class monitor_u has the following determinants:
   |-> has_checker of type bool with value FALSE
```

```
|-> has_checker of type bool with value
    TRUE
|-> has_coverage of type bool with value
    TRUE
```

8.5   Finding method declarations and extensions

PROBLEM   I need to find the declaration and/or the extensions of a method.

SOLUTION   The *e* toolkit provides the following three commands to help you with this:

- ■   **md:** Short for **M**ethod **D**eclaration, this command will find the definition of the named method in the named class;

- ■   **me:** Short for **M**ethod **E**xtensions, this command will find the extensions of the named method in the named class;

- ■   **method:** This command combines the previous two and finds the declaration and the extensions of the named method in the named class.

EXAMPLE   To find the names of all methods in the monitor_u class,

```
etk.pl --show items md monitor_u '.*'
    expecting_overflow
    get_finished_transaction
    monitor
```

To find all extensions to init in any class,

```
etk.pl --show context me '.*' init
    bfm_u::init
    monitor_u::init
```

To find the files where the `drive_transactions` method of the `bfm_u` class is declared or extended,

```
etk.pl --show files method bfm_u drive_transactions
   ./e/bfm.e
```

8.6 Finding field declarations

PROBLEM   I need to find the introduction of a field into a class.

SOLUTION   The *e* toolkit provides the **field** command to help you with this.

EXAMPLE   To find all of the fields in the `monitor_u` class,

```
etk.pl --show items field monitor_u '.*'
   name
   has_checker
   m_finished_transaction
```

or

```
etk.pl --show summary field monitor_u '.*'
   Class, Method, Field, Kind, Type, Start Line,
   End Line, File

   monitor_u, , name, generatable non-physical
   public, env_name_t, 6, 6, ./e/monitor_h.e

   monitor_u, , has_checker, generatable non-
   physical public, bool, 9, 9, ./e/monitor_h.e

   monitor_u, , m_finished_transaction, non-
   generatable(!) non-physical private, alu_
   transaction_s, 25, 25, ./e/monitor.e
```

The first command just returns the names, whereas the second command returns information such as the line number and file name of the declaration, whether the field is public or private, etc.

8.7 Finding event declarations

PROBLEM   I need to find the introduction of an event into a class.

SOLUTION   The *e* toolkit provides the `event` command to help you with
this.

EXAMPLE   To find all of the events in the verification environment,

```
etk.pl --show context event '.*' '.*'
   agent_u::clk
   bfm_u::driver_clock
   monitor_u::clk
   monitor_u::e_transaction_complete
```

I'm using `context` rather than `items,` because I don't just
want all the event names. I also want to know what classes
have events. If two classes have identically named events,
such as `clk`, then `context` will tell me this.

To find all of the clock events in the verification
environment,

```
etk.pl --show context event '.*' 'cl.*'
   agent_u::clk
   monitor_u::clk
```

This assumes all clock events have "`cl`" in them (`clock`, `e_`
`clock`, `clk`, etc.). You might have to do some visual filter-
ing of the results here to ignore superfluous matches.

8.8 Finding enumerated type declarations and extensions

PROBLEM   I need to find the declaration and/or the extensions of an
enumerated type.

SOLUTION   The *e* toolkit provides the following three commands to help you with this:

- **td:** Short for **T**ype **D**eclaration, this command will find the definition of the named enumerated type;

- **te:** Short for **T**ype **E**xtensions, this command will find the extensions of the named enumerated type;

- **type:** This command combines the previous two and finds the declaration and the extensions of the named enumerated type.

EXAMPLE   To find all of the enumerated types in the verification environment,

```
etl.pl --show items td '.*'
   alu_op_t
   env_name_t
   overflow_t
```

8.9   How do I find where a value is added to a type?

PROBLEM   I need to find where a particular value was defined for an enumerated type.

SOLUTION   The *e* toolkit provides the **tvd** command (type value definition) to help you with this.

EXAMPLE   To find all of the values of the alu_op_t type,

```
etk.pl --show items tvd alu_op_t '.*'
   ADD
   SUB
   . . .
```

8.10 Finding cover group declarations and extensions

PROBLEM I need to find the declaration and/or the extensions of a cover group.

SOLUTION The *e* toolkit provides the following three commands to help you with this:

- `covd`: Short for **C**overage **D**eclaration, this command will find the definition of the named coverage group in the named class;

- `cove`: Short for **C**overage **E**xtensions, this command will find the extensions of the named coverage group in the named class;

- `cover`: This command combines the previous two and finds the declaration and the extensions of the named coverage group in the named class.

Note that the name of a coverage group is the name of its sampling event.

EXAMPLE To find the names of all coverage groups in the `monitor_u` class,

```
etk.pl --show items covd monitor_u '.*'
    tr_complete
```

To find all extensions to `tr_complete` in the `monitor_u` class,

```
etk.pl --show summary cove monitor_u tr_complete
    Class, Cover Group, Kind, Start Line, End Line,
    File

    monitor_u, tr_complete, extension (using also),
    65, 65, ./e/coverage.e

    monitor_u, tr_complete using also no_collect,
    extension (is also), 67, 69, ./e/coverage.e
```

To find the files where the `monitor_u` class's `tr_complete` coverage group is defined and/or extended,

```
etk.pl --show files cover monitor_u tr_complete
   ./e/coverage.e
```

8.11 Finding the source of a message in the log file

PROBLEM   I have some text appearing in my log file and I have no idea where it's coming from. How do I find out?

SOLUTION   The *e* toolkit provides the **msg** command (**Message**) to do this for you.

EXAMPLE   To find the source of the following message,

```
[100 ns] VER_VSEQ: Transferring from CPU to SRAM
```

```
etk.pl msg 'Transferring from '.* to .*'
```

DISCUSSION Entries in a log file can come from a number of sources, such as `out()`, `outf()`, `print()`, `message()`, `messagef()`, `error()`, and `dut_error()`. They can also be dynamically generated, either in one go, across multiple statements, or from strings returned from nested methods. This means that finding the source of a message in a log file can take several attempts as you try to latch on to a fragment of the text that exists in the code as it is displayed.

The **msg** command really just performs a regular expression string match against the source code, although comments are not searched. This gives you a great deal of flexibility to specify the match string. It also gives you a chance to pick up false positives.

Let's look at the previous example again.

```
[100 ns] VER_VSEQ: Transferring from CPU to SRAM
```

This looks like it comes from a `message()` command, and it's possible that the `CPU` and `SRAM` words are added dynamically. Therefore, the following search will probably fail:

etk.pl msg 'Transferring from CPU to SRAM'

If it does, you will need to modify your search expression. The following command might help, but by shortening the expression you stand a chance of picking up other messages as well.

etk.pl msg 'Transferring from'

Having a weak search term like this is probably OK, because the message you are looking for should be in the results somewhere. Try to avoid single word searches, because you will start to match real code, such as variable names. For example, if you are looking for the message "`Address = 0x1000_ffff`", then the following command is an obvious one to use, but it will also pick up all fields, properties, coverage items, methods, etc., called `Address`.

etk.pl msg 'Address'

8.12 Finding aspects

Note: This solution only works if you have tagged your aspects using the `aspect start` and `aspect end` tags as described in this section. This is an alternative method of organizing your code than described in "Mapping aspects to files" on page 75, although you can use both concurrently.

PROBLEM   I want to find all of the code belonging to an aspect.

SOLUTION   The *e* toolkit provides the `aspect` command to do this for you. Simply list the tags for all the aspects you want to see, and the toolkit will return the code that is in all of the aspects.

Note that wild cards cannot be used for the aspect names. You have to type them in their entirety.

EXAMPLE   To see all the code that is in the `ahb_slave` and `coverage` aspects,

```
etk.pl aspect ahb_slave coverage
```

DISCUSSION   "Mapping aspects to files," on page 75, discussed how you could structure your code into files to let you find aspects just by using the `ls` and `grep` commands. This is a very useful technique, because you can use these two ubiquitous commands, or even your eyes, to find the files that contain your aspect code.

There are a few downsides to the technique, however:

■ You normally have to start using it when you start coding. It is hard to retrofit to existing code, although not impossible.

■ You have to decide all of your aspects up front. To add a new aspect once the code is written would require you to restructure your files.

■ It can try the patience of those colleagues who can't mentally deal with a lot of files[33] or file names containing more than eight characters.

The *e* toolkit provides an alternative solution to this. Instead of having to structure all of your code into different files that relate to the appropriate aspects, you can structure your code

---

[33] I once had a complaint that I had too many files in my testbench. I had 12! Some people have a ludicrously low threshold for the number of files they can deal with.

in any way you want and just use embedded tags to assign code to aspects. Note that these tags only help you find the code in the aspects. You still need to separate aspects into different files if you want to get the code organization and pluggable code advantages of AOP. Please do not use the tags instead of the techniques introduced in "Mapping aspects to files" on page 75. Use them in addition to those techniques.

The following macros should be used to define the tags:

```
define <etk_aspect_start'statement>       "aspect start <any>" as {{}};
define <etk_aspect_end'statement>         "aspect end   <any>" as {{}};
define <etk_aspect_start'struct_member>   "aspect start <any>" as {{}};
define <etk_aspect_end'struct_member>     "aspect end   <any>" as {{}};
define <etk_aspect_start'action>          "aspect start <any>" as {{}};
define <etk_aspect_end'action>            "aspect end   <any>" as {{}};
```

The macros are defined as statements, struct members, and actions, so you can use them outside classes, inside classes, and inside methods to delimit code. The macros take a space-separated list of aspect names, and these names follow the *e* identifier naming rules.

To show these tags in action, let's use the following example. I'm adding a bus sequence aspect to the configuration interface, and this gives the user a way to modify the verbosity of the bus sequence logger at runtime. To maintain the pluggability benefits of AOP, the new aspect is organized by file. It is stored in bus_seq-config_interface.e. However, the file also instantiates the required logger in the environment and tags the code as belonging to the "config_interface", "bus_sequence", "env", and "logging" aspects, but I don't feel a new file is warranted at this time.[34] Instead of creating a new file, I just add the appropriate tags around the code.

---

[34] By tagging the code, it will be easy to move to a new file later if this is required. The tags will give you the file name.

```
<'
aspect start bus_sequence;
aspect start config_interface;


extend my_evc_config_s {
  // This stores the verbosity of the logger used in the
  // scoreboard base class
  //
  private !bus_seq__logger_verbosity: message_verbosity;


  // This event is triggered when someone changes the verbosity
  // of the bus sequence logger using the bus_seq_logger_
  // verbosity() method.
  //
  event e_bus_seq__logger_verbosity_changed;


  // Call this method to set the verbosity of the logger used
  // by the scoreboard base class.
  //
  bus_seq__logger_verbosity (v: message_verbosity) is{
    bus_seq__logger_verbosity = v;


    log_change("bus_seq__logger_verbosity", v.as_a(string));
    emit e_bus_seq__logger_verbosity_changed;
  };


  // Call this method to get the verbosity of the logger used
  // by the scoreboard base class.
  //
  bus_seq__what_is_the_logger_verbosity(): message_verbosity is{
    result = bus_seq__logger_verbosity;
  };
```

```
  init() is also{
    bus_seq__logger_verbosity = FULL;
  };
};

aspect start logging;

extend message_tag : [BUS_SEQ_LOGGER];

aspect start env;


extend my_env_u{
  // A bus sequence logger
  //
  logger_bus_seq : message_logger is instance;
  keep soft logger_bus_seq.to_screen == TRUE;
  keep soft logger_bus_seq.tags == {BUS_SEQ_LOGGER};


  event e_bus_seq__logger_verbosity_changed is
     @config.e_bus_seq__logger_verbosity_changed;


  on e_bus_seq__logger_verbosity_changed{
    outf("Changing the Bus Sequence Logger to %s\n",
        config.bus_seq__what_is_the_logger_verbosity()
    );
    logger_bus_seq.set_actions(
      config.bus_seq__what_is_the_logger_verbosity(),
        {BUS_SEQ_LOGGER}, "*", "...", replace);
  };
};


aspect end logging env;
aspect end bus_sequence config_interface;
'>
```

Code Listing 63. Using tags to mark an aspect.

This code sample shows that the tags can be nested and can have multiple aspects listed per tag. The next few examples are based on some bigger code that I've not included in the book. To see all the files that are involved in the config_ interface aspect, you would type

```
etk.pl --show files aspect config_interface
   ./bus_seq-config_interface.e
   ./env-config_interface.e
   ./end_of_test-config_interface.e
   ./scoreboard-config_interface.e
   ./config_interface.e
```

To see all the code in the env aspect, type

```
etk.pl --show all aspect env
```

```
.-------------+---------------------------------------
|             | Aspect       : env
|             | File         : ./bus_seq-config_int...
|    Lines    |              : 38 to 59
+-------------+---------------------------------------
|             |
| [ 38 -  38] |   aspect start logging env;
| [ 40 -  40] |   extend message_tag : [BUS_SEQ_LO...
| [ 42 -  42] |   extend my_env_u{
| [ 44 -  44] |       logger_bus_seq : message_logg...
| [ 45 -  45] |       keep soft logger_bus_seq.to_s...
| [ 46 -  46] |       keep soft logger_bus_seq.tags...
| [ 48 -  48] |       event e_bus_seq__logger_verbo...
| [ 50 -  50] |       on e_bus_seq__logger_verbosit...
| [ 51 -  52] |         outf("**** Changing the ve...
| [ 54 -  55] |         logger_bus_seq.set_actions...
| [ 56 -  56] |       };
| [ 57 -  57] |     };
| [ 59 -  59] |   aspect end bus_sequence config_i...
`-------------+---------------------------------------
```

```
.-------------+------------------------------------
|             | Aspect       : env
|             | File         : ./env-config_interfa...
|    Lines    |              : 3 to 7
+-------------+------------------------------------
|             |
| [  3 -   3] | aspect start env config_interface;
| [  4 -   4] | extend my_env_u{
| [  5 -   5] |    config: my_evc_config_s;
| [  6 -   6] | };
| [  7 -   7] | aspect end env config_interface;
|             |
`-------------+------------------------------------


.-------------+------------------------------------
|             | Aspect       : env
|             | File         : ./env.e
|    Lines    |              : 3 to 7
+-------------+------------------------------------
|             |
| [  3 -   3] | aspect start env;
| [  5 -   5] | unit my_env_u{};
| [  7 -   7] | aspect end env;
|             |
`-------------+------------------------------------
```

To see all the code in both the logging and the env aspect
(from a bigger example), type

`etk.pl --show all aspect logging env`

```
.-------------+------------------------------------
|             | Aspect       : env
|             | File         : ./bus_seq-config_int...
|    Lines    |              : 38 to 59
+-------------+------------------------------------
|             |
| [ 38 -  38] | aspect start logging env;
| [ 40 -  40] | extend message_tag : [BUS_SEQ_LO...
| [ 42 -  42] | extend my_env_u{
| [ 44 -  44] |    logger_bus_seq : message_logg...
```

```
|  [ 45 -  45]  |      keep soft logger_bus_seq.to_s...
|  [ 46 -  46]  |      keep soft logger_bus_seq.tags...
|  [ 48 -  48]  |      event e_bus_seq__logger_verbo...
|  [ 50 -  50]  |      on e_bus_seq__logger_verbosit...
|  [ 51 -  52]  |         outf("**** Changing the ve...
|  [ 54 -  55]  |         logger_bus_seq.set_actions...
|  [ 56 -  56]  |      };
|  [ 57 -  57]  |   };
|  [ 59 -  59]  |   aspect end bus_sequence config_i...
|              |
`-------------+-------------------------------------
```

Bibliography

[1] P. Graham, *Beating the Averages*, April 2001, rev. April 2003, www.paulgraham.com/avg.html

[2] S. Garfinkel, D. Weise, and S. Strassmann, *The UNIX Haters Handbook*, 1994, research.microsoft.com/~daniel/unix-haters.html

[3] A. J. Perlis, "Epigrams in Programming," *ACM, SIGPLAN Notices* vol. 17, no. 9, pages 7–13, September 1982.

[4] G. Kiczales, J. Lamping, A. Mendhekar, C. Maeda, C. Lopes, J.-M. Loingtier, and J. Irwin, *Aspect-Oriented Programming*, ECOOP '97, 1997.

[5] P. Ng and I. Jacobson, *Aspect-Oriented Software Development with Use Cases*, Reading, MA: Addison–Wesley, 2005.

[6] C. Lopes, *Aspect Oriented Programming: A Historical Perspective (What's in a Name?)*, Institute for Software Research Technical Report UCI-ISR-02-5, 2002.

[7] Y. Hollander, M. Morley, and A. Noy, *The e Language: A Fresh Separation of Concerns*, TOOLS Europe, 2001.

[8] M. Völter, *Handling Cross-Cutting Concerns: AOP and Beyond*, 2003, www.voelter.de/publications/index/detail723358759.html

[9] A. Holub, *Why Extends Is Evil*, Java World, 2003, www.javaworld.com/javaworld/jw-08-2003/jw-0801-toolbox.html

[10] S. C. Johnson *Objecting to Objects*, www.usenix.org/publications/library/proceedings/sf94/full_papers/johnson.html

[11] D. Robinson, J. Sprott, and G. Allan, *Learn to do Verification with AOP? We've Just Learned OOP!*, SNUG, 2004. www.verilab.com

[12] H. Ossher and P. Tarr, "Multi-Dimensional Separation of Concerns and the Hyperspace Approach," Symposium

on Software Architectures and Component Technology, 2000.

[13]   Talin, *Encapsulation, Inheritance and the Platypus Effect*, May 2000, www.advogato.org/article/83.html

[14]   M. Kircher, P. Jain, and A. Corsaro, *XP + AOP = Better Software?*, XP2002, 2002.

[15]   *Aspects*, www.webopedia.com/TERM/A/aspects.html

[16]   J. Spolsky, *REALBasic*, www.joelonsoftware.com/articles/fog0000000051.html

[17]   I. Jacobson, *The Case for Aspects*, www.jaczone.com/papers/10sd.Jacobson32-37.pdf, 2003.

[18]   J. Spolsky, *Working on CityDesk, Part Three*, www.joelonsoftware.com/articles/fog0000000006.html

[19]   F. Brooks, *The Mythical Man-Month: Essays on Software Engineering*, Reading, MA: Addison–Wesley, 1995.

[20]   E. Gamma, R. Helm, R. Johnson, and J. Vlissides, *Design Patterns: Elements of Reusable Object-Oriented Software*, Reading, MA: Addison–Wesley Professional, 1995.

[21]   M. Feathers, *Working Effectively with Legacy Code*, New York: Prentice Hall PTR, 2004.

Epilogue

And I thought I had finished writing this thing.

Me

Before you put this book down and get back to what you were doing earlier, I just wanted to share this example with you because I think it shows the pragmatic advantages of AOP perfectly. It isn't a contrived example — it turned up one day on a client project and needed a solution very quickly. The AOP solution is simple, but I still can't think how I would have solved this without AOP.

I needed to add support to my verification environment to generically handle address access violations. An address access violation is when someone tries to access an address without using the proper security mechanism. Perhaps the access needs to be in privileged mode; perhaps a sideband signal has to be asserted; perhaps a special value has to have been written to a password register first; perhaps all of these; perhaps something else entirely.

I needed to set up my verification environment in such a way that the end user could check any generic scheme. They needed to be able to configure the scoreboards to check every access to see whether it was allowed. If it wasn't allowed, an error should have been returned from the slave. The problem was that I couldn't modify the scoreboard.

The AOP solution was simple. I added an `is also` extension to the scoreboard's `compare()` method, and this checked for some standard violations and then called a hook, which the end user could extend multiple times to deal with any scenario he or she wanted. This was done without having to modify the original code at all.

The AOP solution was trivial. An OOP solution turned out to be impossible. Because the original author hadn't inserted a hook at the appropriate place, I couldn't use the functor or hook class based approaches discussed in "Reducing the OOP-induced overhead" on page 155. Instead, the only possible solution was to use inheritance to try to overload the `compare()` method. If you ignore for a moment the fact that `compare()` wasn't declared as virtual (which means this approach won't work), the problem was getting the verification environment to use the new type. Scoreboards were automatically created, so I would have to create new ones, initialize them manually, and coerce the verification environment into using them. That was impossible as well, because some of the references to the scoreboards were private and couldn't be changed.

So there you go — a trivial AOP solution or an impossible OOP solution. What would you prefer on your project? I've discussed possible OOP solutions for this with several people now, and they have all boiled down to this:

> *if the original designers had put a hook in, then it would be easy.*

They are probably right; *if* the original designers had predicted this need *and* they had put the appropriate infrastructure in place, then it would be easy to solve.

But they didn't, so it wasn't. For me, this is the real advantage of AOP. AOP makes it easy to work with real-world verification environments. OOP on its own doesn't.

Have fun ....

Index

www.ingramcontent.com/pod-product-compliance
Lightning Source LLC
Chambersburg PA
CBHW082110220326
41598CB00066BA/6024